A dream is real so long as it lasts. When we awake, we do not pass from unreality to reality; we pass from a lower state of reality to a higher one. Is it not possible that there is a state of awareness higher still, compared with which the limited satisfactions of everyday life are no more lasting than a dream?

EKNATH EASWARAN

COMPANION VOLUMES

PASSAGE MEDITATION
Bringing the Deep Wisdom
of the Heart into Daily Life

TIMELESS WISDOM
Passages for Meditation from the
World's Saints & Sages

The Mantram Handbook

A Practical Guide to Choosing Your Mantram & Calming Your Mind

EKNATH EASWARAN

Foreword by Daniel H. Lowenstein, MD

 NILGIRI PRESS

Fifth edition. First printing January 2009

ISBN: 978-1-58638-028-1

Library of Congress Control Number: 2008931228

Printed on 100% postconsumer recycled paper

Publisher's Cataloging-in-Publication block

will be found on the last leaf of this book.

Eknath Easwaran founded the Blue Mountain Center of Meditation
in Berkeley, California, in 1961. The Center is a nonprofit organization
chartered with carrying on Easwaran's legacy and work. Nilgiri Press,
a department of the Center, publishes books on how to lead a spiritual
life in the home and community. The Center also teaches Easwaran's
eight-point program of passage meditation at retreats worldwide.

For information please visit www.easwaran.org,

call us at 800 475 2369 (USA)

or 707 878 2369 (international and local),

or write to us at The Blue Mountain Center of Meditation,

Box 256, Tomales, CA 94971-0256, USA.

Table of Contents

The Brain, the Mind, & the Mantram

By Daniel H. Lowenstein, MD

AS A PHYSICIAN and neuroscientist, I tend to gaze at human behavior through the lenses of biology. Four billion years of evolutionary trial and error have led to the creation of this magnificent entity we call the brain, the physical source of our behavior and the seat of our individual consciousness. The collective good that has been wrought by this extraordinary network of cells and connections – the most complex physical entity in the known universe – is staggering. When singularly focused on an idea or task, our brain and mind have a limitless capacity to explore, solve, and create.

And yet, as I watch the ways of people, as I listen to my patients' stories, as I share observations with friends and colleagues, grocery clerks and taxi drivers, as I contemplate my own fifty-plus years of conscious awareness, I am struck by the ongoing parade of conflicts and challenges and mental strife. How many of us can recall a week, let alone a day, where we were not wrestling with something that was the source of psychic discomfort? We fear failure. We are swept with irritation and impatience, with anxiety over events that have yet to occur, and with disappointment over events that have already occurred. We carry guilt, worry, and discontent about our health, our accomplishments, our bodies, our memory, our parenting skills. Interspersed in this negative stream are random thoughts that erupt and sweep our consciousness: a sudden craving for pizza, a vision of ourselves in a new, attractive sweater, a longing to visit Hawaii, a replay of a conversation from yesterday. The list seems endless!

Why does this happen? Why does our consciousness flow like a relentless deluge of bothersome or nonproductive thoughts, when our brain and mind have the capacity to bring a laser focus to a single task?

Modern neuroscience has begun to reveal the biological underpinning of parts of our consciousness. We now understand, for example, that the emotional experience of fear requires the activation of the amygdala, a small, globular collection of neurons (nerve cells) located deep inside the temporal lobe. The perception of conflict, whether internal or external, involves a stretch of brain along the midline known as the anterior cingulate. The orbitofrontal cortex, located at the very front part of the brain, has a critical role in weighing reward and punishment, which is the basis of decision-making.

Yet, despite these advances, we still have no understanding about the nature of the recurrent and unsatisfying thoughts that distract our mind. Zen teachings refer to this as the "monkey mind," as if there were a troop of mischievous monkeys jumping and bouncing between every corner of our consciousness.

And this is just at the surface of our brain activity; these are the thoughts of which we are "aware." We all recognize that there is a realm of mind at the subconscious and unconscious levels, but few appreciate just how vast this realm must be. As one simple but graphic example, consider how we use vision to perceive the world. What constitutes the experience of "seeing"? In fact, we are *not* limited to items that enter our conscious awareness. We know this in part because of the discovery of a remarkable phenomenon called blindsight. There are rare individuals who, as a result of injury to specific regions of their visual cortex at the back of the brain, have lost their capacity to see. This is a special kind of blindness that is present in a small percentage of blind people. The blindsighted see nothing, just as you see nothing from the back of your own head. Now let's try the following experiment. We tell the blindsighted person that we are going to test his vision by holding our hands up in front of him and briefly moving the fingers of our right or left hand. We then ask this person which hand is moving. Our test subject protests, "Don't waste your time. I cannot see anything!" To which we respond: "We understand – but just do your best. It may feel like you are guessing, but you need to choose right or left." The experiment begins, and, amazingly, the subject is able to choose the correct side each time.

Is this surprising? Perhaps it is not. Why should we assume that vision is only limited to those perceptions that enter our conscious awareness? In fact, our visual system is processing a huge amount of sensory information that strikes the eyes but never bubbles up to the surface of our conscious experience of seeing the world. Now take this one step further. If there is a realm of brain activity below the surface that is dedicated to something as relatively simple as analyzing the light patterns that strike our eyes, what about all the other activities of the brain and the mind?

Which brings me to the mantram.

By chance – almost twenty years ago – I met Eknath Easwaran. He was interested in the world of medicine and the workings of the mind. In exchange for my medical consultation he gave me a copy of his book *Meditation,* which I carefully placed on my nightstand and forgot. Fortunately, my wife picked it up and gradually helped me and our children to appreciate the wisdom of this remarkable man. Over the years, I had numerous conversations with Easwaran, attended retreats at the Blue Mountain Center of Meditation, and began to recognize the brilliance of his ability to distill and convey the essence of the world's great spiritual traditions. His "eightfold body of spiritual disciplines," described in chapter 11 of this book, is an elegant, logical, and practical approach for finding fulfillment and peace in everyday living.

As Easwaran emphasizes, it is important to consider all eight of these disciplines together, rather than as separate practices from which to pick and choose. However, of the eight practices, I have found the mantram to be powerfully transformative yet simplest to use. In this book, Eknath Easwaran explains how to use the mantram by silently repeating a few words from one of the great spiritual traditions, words like "Om mani padme hum" or "Ave Maria."

The mantram works specifically as an antidote to the daily conflicts and intrusions filling our unquiet minds. At the most superficial level, repetition of the mantram causes the brain to swing from barely connected thoughts to a simple phrase that holds the attention and thus slows down the mind. The science of neurobiology gives another way to understand how the mantram could be working. From studies using magnetic resonance imaging (MRI), we know that concentrating on a short phrase will activate specific areas in the front and side of the brain. These areas, the frontal and parietal lobes, are involved in selective attention – the capacity to maintain a single focus despite the presence of distracting stimuli. In this way, the mental repetition of a simple phrase like a mantram can provide a guidewire to move your attention away from a troubling stream of thoughts. It is as though the mantram provides access to a peaceful, grounded center that puts our cravings, drives, and other immediate needs in perspective.

Does the mantram also work on deeper levels of consciousness? In my own experience, I have seen that it does. After I had repeated the mantram consciously over a period of time, I found the words arising naturally when I faced a situation of fear or distress. In fact, now I sometimes become aware of the mantram repeating itself *before* I actually realize that I am in a predicament. This type of brain learning, where an act frequently repeated becomes an unconscious activity, is related to the recruitment of more and more neurons in brain regions that are activated by unconscious as well as conscious activity. Thus a skilled soccer player sees an opening and kicks a perfect goal without thinking consciously about the force required or the correct angle. Thus you and I – having learned to ride a bicycle – use our body to steer, move forward, and brake properly without conscious thought.

Yet other questions remain. Why does there seem to be a need for a mantram that has spiritual roots? Are there even deeper levels of consciousness that the mantram can reach? Are there any negatives to relying on a mantram? Neuroscience currently lacks answers for these questions, and I suspect this will be the case for a very long time, if not forever. However, historically there's no doubt that the mantram has been a powerful and positive tool – great spiritual teachers like the Buddha and Mahatma Gandhi have used mantrams extensively on their spiritual journeys.

Ultimately, one must rely on experience to measure the success of any activity. I can attest to the value of the mantram in everyday life. It instantly creates a grounding that helps clear away the extraneous activities of mind – conscious and, I believe, unconscious. It enables me to be slower, more focused, more aware, and more connected. I say the mantram before every patient visit in my clinic. I say it before every teaching experience. I say it when I feel myself becoming impatient, or angry, or dismayed. And though I am probably lifetimes away from realizing its full potential, there is no question that the mantram has altered the everyday function of my brain and mind in a way that has made life even more enriching and fulfilling.

Now it is your turn to take up the lens of the skeptical scientist. Do your own experiments. As Eknath Easwaran says, try using the mantram in your daily life, and see what happens!

Preface

I HAVE WRITTEN THIS BOOK because I want to share with you a simple spiritual practice that you can begin to use today, no matter what your situation, to tap your deeper resources in all the ups and downs of daily life. It doesn't require any special gifts, and you don't need to follow any systematic program. You can begin using and benefiting from this simple spiritual practice, called a mantram, right now.

You can use it anytime, anywhere. And it works.

Over a long period of time, the mantram can bring about far-reaching changes in your state of mind, gradually elevating your consciousness. This appeals to many people, but most of us are looking for something we can use and benefit from right now. So this book offers a kind of first aid for the mind and the emotions.

Using a mantram is so simple that I can tell you in a few brief paragraphs exactly how to start using this powerful tool today.

HOW TO USE A MANTRAM

A *mantram* – or *mantra,* as it is often called* – is a powerful spiritual formula, which, when repeated silently in the mind, has the capacity to transform consciousness. There is nothing magical about this. It is simply a matter of practice. The mantram is a short, powerful spiritual formula for the highest power that we can conceive of – whether we call it God, or the ultimate reality, or the Self within. Whatever name we use, with the mantram we are calling up what is best and deepest in ourselves. The mantram has appeared in every major spiritual tradition, West and East, because it fills a deep, universal need in the human heart.

Select a mantram that appeals to you. Every religious tradition has a mantram, often more than one. But you needn't subscribe to any religion to benefit from the mantram – you simply have to be willing to try it. For Christians, the name of Jesus itself is a powerful mantram; Catholics also use *Hail Mary* or *Ave Maria.* Jews may use *Barukh attah Adonai;* Muslims use the name of Allah or *Bismillah ir-Rahman ir-Rahim.* Probably the oldest Buddhist mantram is *Om mani padme hum.* And in Hinduism, among many choices, I recommend *Rama, Rama,* which was Mahatma Gandhi's mantram. A list of mantrams, with background for each, begins on page 33.

Once you have chosen your mantram, do not change it. If

---

* *Mantram* and *mantra* are different forms of the same Sanskrit word. Both are correct.

you do, you will be like a person digging shallow holes in many places; you will never go deep enough to find water.

The mantram is most effective when repeated silently in the mind. You don't have to chant it aloud, and it doesn't require any fixed times or place or special equipment. Repeat your mantram silently whenever you get the chance: while walking, while waiting, while doing mechanical chores such as washing dishes, and especially when you are falling asleep. You will find that this is not mindless repetition; the mantram will help to keep you relaxed and alert during the day, and when you can fall asleep in it, it will go on working for you throughout the night as well.

Whenever you are angry or afraid, nervous or worried or resentful, repeat the mantram until the agitation subsides. The mantram works to steady the mind, and all these emotions are power running against you which the mantram can harness and put to work for you.

Finally, the mantram relates to a larger body of spiritual disciplines: proven techniques which we can all put into practice to make our lives richer, more purposeful and fulfilling. With these techniques, beginning with meditation, we can harness the immense resources within us to unify our personality and make a lasting contribution to life, knowing every day that we are needed and cherished by those around us.

This is the real glory of the human being, that we can choose to remake ourselves completely.

The chapters that follow elucidate the above instructions, supporting you in your practice of the mantram. But nothing I can tell you will have as much meaning as using the mantram for yourself. If you use it, you will know its power.

CHAPTER ONE

Initiation into the Mantram

IN MY COLLEGE days in India, I was on the debating team, and I enjoyed debating very much. I enjoyed preparing ahead of time to present both sides of the issues that the debating masters proposed. And, when facing a well-spoken and well-prepared opponent, I enjoyed the intensity of debate itself. For me, it had all the drama of an athletic event, with its possibilities for mastery of a difficult skill and for grace under pressure. What I didn't like, however, was the feeling of intense stage fright that I felt for about an hour before each debate was to begin. During that hour, I suffered all the well-known symptoms of this common malady: sweaty palms, irregular breathing, a pounding heart, and, worst of all, the question that would go through my mind over and over: Why did I ever join the debating society? And the anguished answer: I wish I never had! I can't go through with this; I *can't* go through with this.

I was a young Hindu boy from a small village in Kerala State, South India, and it was my first year at a Catholic college where English was the medium of instruction. All debating was, of course, done in English. I had studied English in my high school, but it was not my native language, and in fact none of my high school teachers were native speakers of English. Needless to say, I felt insecure about my abilities to speak English on the debating platform with boys who, though also using English as a second language, had been brought up in the town, where they heard British speakers of English. Many had also come from schools where English had been the medium of instruction all along.

More subtly, I was a Hindu – a minority among a large majority of Catholics. It was not that I felt discriminated against. The head of the Catholic college went out of his way to see that I received every opportunity open to me. Yet, in those days of British rule in India, it was taken for granted that Western culture was superior – that a Christian, though an Indian, might naturally be expected to have an advantage over his Hindu brother.

There I was, just starting my college career, with a love for public speaking and especially for debating, about to give it all up because I couldn't bear that hour of terror before stepping up onto the platform. Yes, it was unreasonable; but it seemed an obstacle I just couldn't overcome.

Then I went to my grandmother, my spiritual teacher, and asked her what to do about the anxiety that gripped me whenever I had to stand and speak before an audience. She told me not to dwell on the anxiety, but just to keep repeating in my mind the words *Rama, Rama, Rama*. I knew this was a mantram that my granny used. When I was a child, I used to wake up every morning in our spacious ancestral home to the sweet sound of her singing her mantram as she swept the courtyard with her coconut fiber broom. At that time I didn't give the mantram much thought; it was just something I heard every morning from the lips of someone I loved very deeply.

So I knew that *Rama* was used as a prayer or mantram, but I wasn't a particularly devout young man, and my unspoken reaction to my granny's advice was, "That's too easy, too simple, too miraculous." I was skeptical, but such was my love for my grandmother that I tried it anyway. "I hope it works," I said, and the next time I sat on the platform waiting my turn to speak, I kept repeating the mantram in my mind. It seemed to help.

After that, whenever I was called upon to debate, I would silently repeat the mantram beforehand, and after a while I said, "I think it works." I would still get a few butterflies in my stomach, but I no longer suffered from a pounding heart and irregular breathing.

Then I began to use it on any occasion that I found stressful. Today, after many years of using the mantram, I can say, on the strength of my own personal experience, "I *know* it works."

Thanks to the wisdom of my grandmother, I enjoyed debating throughout my college career, which was crowned by the day our team won the intercollegiate debating championship. Later in life, also due to her blessings, I have enjoyed two careers involving public speaking: one as a college professor of English and one as a teacher of meditation. And I have never been paralysed by stage fright, all because I followed her simple advice to "just repeat *Rama, Rama, Rama.*"

THE POWER OF THE MANTRAM

Many years ago, after I took to meditation, I started treasuring every moment that I could repeat the mantram. I did not undertake these practices out of frustration: by Indian standards, I was successful and had everything that was thought to be desirable in life. But just at this hour of fulfillment, all these things no longer satisfied me. The ground shifted under my feet, and I turned inward. It was then that I began to repeat the mantram in earnest, using it everywhere during the day and at night. Two minutes here while on my way to class, two there while waiting at the bank, two minutes there waiting for the bus, five minutes there waiting in a restaurant – I don't think I wasted many opportunities.

All of this did not come naturally to me. I was not noted for devotion in my early life. I had come from a very deeply religious family, but I was more interested in the modern world and came under the influence of Western culture very early in life. Yet it was my enormous good fortune, when I began to face the storms that life is full of, that I could remember my grandmother's unshakable strength and begin to rely on her mantram myself. Since then, every day has brought a deeper realization of the mantram's power to turn fear into fearlessness, anger into compassion, and hatred into love.

After many, many years there comes a day when you are

delivered from the turmoil of the mind and the mantram is with you all the time. Then no insecurity can come into your heart. No ill will can come into your mind. You can go into any situation, and you won't get upset. You won't be overwhelmed. You will be able to give your very best and you will be at your very best, whatever the circumstances.

This was my goal: to repeat the mantram so long and so often that it would become established in my consciousness. Today I don't have to make an effort to repeat the mantram. It goes on all the time. The benefits are enormous, and I will be telling you about them later in this book.

THE POWER OF TRADITION

All the great religions have produced powerful spiritual formulas which are the highest symbol of the supreme reality we call God. In the Catholic tradition, and many other traditions in both East and West, such a formula is called a holy name; in Hinduism and Buddhism, it is called a mantram. The holy name stands for that supreme power of which Saint John asserts: "In the beginning was the Word, and the Word was with God, and the Word was God." A very simple and devoted man of God, Swami Ramdas, whom my wife and I had the blessing of meeting in India, tells us very much the same thing when he says, "The Name *is* God."

The mental repetition of the holy name is one of the simplest and most effective ways of practicing the presence of God, to use the phrase of the seventeenth-century French mystic, Brother Lawrence. It is absolutely practical, and it can appeal to our common sense. When we repeat the mantram, we are not hypnotizing ourselves, or woolgathering, or turning our backs on the world. Repetition of the mantram is a dynamic discipline by which we gain access to our inner reserves of strength and peace of mind. With the mantram we regain our natural energy, confidence, and control, so that we can transform everything negative in us and make our greatest possible contribution to the welfare of those around us.

The mantram is the living symbol of the profoundest reality that the human being can conceive of, the highest power that we can respond to and love. When we repeat the mantram in our mind, we are reminding ourselves of this supreme reality enshrined in our hearts. It is only natural that the more we repeat the mantram, the deeper it will sink into our consciousness. As it goes deeper, it will strengthen our will, heal the old divisions in our consciousness that now cause us conflict and turmoil, and give us access to deeper resources of strength, patience, and love, to work for the benefit of all.

"The mantram becomes one's staff of life," declares Mahatma Gandhi, "and carries one through every ordeal."

So, my advice is simple and direct: when you are faced with an overwhelming challenge or simply a difficult situation, repeat *Rama, Rama, Rama,* or whatever other mantram you have chosen (see chapter 3). Just try it and see.

IT'S NOT MIRACULOUS

There is nothing miraculous about the power of the mantram. When you repeat the holy name you are calling on the Self in your own heart, and that Self will give you access to your own deeper resources.

This is not something you do for two minutes one day and then give up if results are not immediately forthcoming – although even a little repetition of the mantram is helpful. If you call on God long enough and sincerely enough, he or she cannot help responding. I saw a graphic illustration of this once when my wife and I were walking in Berkeley near the campus and chanced upon the final scene of a lover's quarrel. The young lady must have given her boyfriend his hat, told him that she never wanted to see him again, and pushed him out the door. He stood there on the sidewalk and began to call her name: "Cynthia, Cynthia." He shouted it louder and louder and soon the whole block was echoing with "Cynthia! Cynthia! Cynthia!" Passersby were staring, the neighbors were coming out of their houses to see what was going on, and dogs began to howl. Finally Cynthia opened an upstairs window and told him, "All right! *All right!* I'm coming down!" In just the same way, sincere and systematic use of the holy name can bring a deeper power, a divine presence, to play in our own lives.

Instead of just saying the mantram once, the way we say hello at the beginning of a conversation, the idea is to repeat it over and over again, and to use every chance throughout the day for repeating it more. In all the great religions there have been mystics who have become so established in the mantram that they would be plunged into a deeper level of consciousness by hearing the holy name just once. But this is not likely to happen when we are just beginning to use it. The effect of the mantram is cumulative: constant repetition, constant practice, is required for the mantram to take root in our consciousness and gradually transform it, just as constant repetition makes the advertiser's jingle stick in our minds. This may sound tedious, but it is far from that. The mantram soon becomes a familiar friend of whom we never grow tired.

KEEP IT SIMPLE

The mantram is most effective when we say it silently, in the mind, with as much concentration as possible. Sometimes saying the mantram aloud a few times can help you get it started in the mind, and it is so rhythmical that it can be sung aloud, as it often is in many religious traditions. Some of my friends even confess to singing it in the shower.

But by and large I recommend repeating the mantram silently, and not dwelling on tune and rhythm and such matters. Anything which takes attention away from the mantram itself, such as counting or worrying about intonation or connecting the mantram with physiological processes, only weakens the mantram's effect; it is like trying to dive to the bottom of a swimming pool when you have an inner tube around your waist. So it is best right from the outset not to get dependent on external aids, not even the rosary that is used in many religious traditions. After a short while, any such aid is of little use, and eventually it will even hold you back. Counting or thinking about what your hands are doing only helps keep you on the surface level of awareness; it may even encourage your repetition to become mechanical.

Similarly, let me urge you not to connect the repetition of the mantram with your breathing or your heartbeat. There is no harm if this happens of its own accord, but in making a conscious effort to link the mantram with these rhythms, you may interfere with vital processes which the body, with its native wisdom, is already regulating at optimum efficiency.

A mantram is more than just a word or phrase; it is a force, and in order for this force to heal the divisions in our consciousness and to give us access to our deeper resources, it must be working from deep inside. At first, of course, we will be repeating the mantram only at the surface level of the mind. But if we repeat it with regularity and sustained enthusiasm, it will take root deep in our consciousness until it becomes as natural to us as breathing.

There is nothing mysterious about this process. We all have the capacity to concentrate, especially on things we like, and concentration itself is a deeper level of awareness. When we get absorbed in an intricate problem, or in reading our favorite author, or in listening to music we love, or in doing anything else that commands our full attention, we are no longer aware of our surroundings or of extraneous sights and sounds; we may not even be aware of our body. In moments of intense concentration like these, we experience a deeper level of awareness. It is just the same with the mantram; it can come from a level beyond awareness of sights and sounds, beyond awareness of the body, even beyond the level of words and conceptual thought.

Sometimes, in the West as well as in the East, you hear that the mantram is only effective if repeated in a particular way – with exactly the right pronunciation and intonation, or a set number of times. Let me assure you that any way you say it, the mantram works. Whether you say it fast or slow, with an Oxford accent or a Tennessee drawl, for five minutes or for hours at a stretch, you are still repeating the name of the Self, who is waiting to be discovered in the depths of your consciousness.

CHAPTER TWO

Choosing a Mantram

WHATEVER RELIGION YOU profess, or if you profess
no religion, you can still use the mantram. Many people
today want to avoid religious connotations and associations,
and I can sympathize with that. But I encourage such people
not to deprive themselves of the inner strength that a rich
spiritual tradition can bring. In a book applying some of the
techniques of meditation to medical problems, a well-known
doctor from this country suggests using the word *one* as a
mantram. The author's intent was to avoid any reference to
religion altogether, which is not inappropriate, since meditation is a technique rather than a religion. But as I read his sug-
gestions I recalled that in the most ancient Hindu scriptures,
God is said to be *advaita*, "One without a second." Plotinus, a
Western mystic of the third century, calls the Godhead simply
"the One," and the beautiful Jewish confession of faith, the
Shema, begins, "Hear, O Israel; the Lord our God, the Lord is
one." So, even when we try to avoid religious associations, it
is good to realize that they are universal, and that we can use
them for our own spiritual growth in the way that is best for us.

Exercise some care in your choice of a mantram. It is important to take into account your own background, your response to the meaning, and the practical significance of the words. Choose a mantram from one of the established traditions, a mantram recommended by a spiritual teacher with personal experience of its power.

Take your time choosing a mantram. You may want to finish reading chapter 3, which lists many suitable mantrams, before making your choice. Then, once you have chosen a mantram, do not change it.

THE OPEN HAND

There are two schools where the giving of a mantram is concerned. In what I playfully call the cloak-and-dagger school, you are taken into a little room, the light is switched off, and a voice whispers in your ear, "Here is your mantram. Don't reveal it to a soul." This is one way, and there are people who respond to it; it is the right way for them, and I have no quarrel with it. But there is another school of thought which is a little more my style, represented by a great mystic of South India named Ramanuja.

When Ramanuja was a spiritual aspirant, just beginning on the spiritual path, he was given his mantram by a very orthodox teacher who told him in the orthodox manner, "Don't breathe a word of this to anybody." Ramanuja didn't see what all the mystery was about, and he asked, "What will happen if I *do* reveal my mantram to someone else?" His teacher told him, "Everyone who hears it will get the benefit, but you will be barred from salvation." When Ramanuja heard this, he went straight to the temple, climbed to the top of the highest tower, and called everyone in the village. "I know a mantram which will make you all secure and selfless," he told them, and he shouted his mantram again and again for everyone to hear. When his spiritual teacher heard about this, he pretended to be angry and scolded Ramanuja severely. But Ramanuja replied calmly, "If my damnation can alleviate the suffering of so many, it is a very small price to pay." It was an answer that must have pleased his teacher greatly.

This approach is one which the Buddha would call "the way of the open hand." The spiritual teacher says, "I don't have a closed fist; my hand is open. Everything I know that can help you cross the sea of life is yours for the asking." You can select the mantram that suits you best. But there is a responsibility which goes along with this approach: you must choose your mantram wisely, according to your deepest needs. If you respond deeply to Jesus, then *Jesus, Jesus* is the right mantram for you. If you respond deeply to the Virgin Mary, then *Hail Mary* is a good mantram for you. If you respond deeply to the Lord as the source of abiding joy, *Rama, Rama* is the right mantram for you. Chapter 3 will tell you more about these and other mantrams, so that you can choose one for yourself.

A FEW CAUTIONS

You may respond to a mantram because of your childhood background, but there is a danger here, too; some people are allergic to particular holy names for the very same reason. Here I get practical. If it is going to take a number of years of repetition just to make you like the mantram, and then more years to make the mantram part of your consciousness, it is a matter of simple economy to choose a mantram about which you have no reservations. So if you have difficulties with the mantram appropriate to your background, you might use *Rama, Rama* or the Buddhist mantram *Om mani padme hum*, which makes no direct reference to God at all.

Be wary of choosing a mantram *just* because it's exotic. The name of Allah may conjure up visions of date palms and camels with tinkling bells; this appeals to some people, and they say, "*Allah, Allah* is the mantram for me." The trouble with this kind of appeal is that after a few weeks, date palms begin to cloy, and you find yourself wanting to change to some other mantram.

I wouldn't suggest making up your own mantram, either. More than once I have had rugged individualists come to me and say, "I'd like to use *peace, peace, peace* as my mantram." *Peace* is a beautiful word, I agree, but not just any beautiful word will do as a mantram. Choose a mantram of proven power, one which has enabled many men and women before you to realize for themselves the unity of life. The roots of such a mantram are far deeper than we can know when we first begin to use it, and this is what enables it to grow in our consciousness.

Use a mantram recommended by a spiritual teacher; you can be sure that it will be charged with the teacher's own personal experience of the mantram's power. All of the mantrams which I recommend are mantrams of proven power, bequeathed to us by the great spiritual teachers of many traditions. In chapter 3 you will find a more detailed list of mantrams, and something of the background of each one.

If no one mantram appeals to you more than any other, I would recommend *Rama, Rama,* one of the oldest, simplest, and most powerful of mantrams. Often, people who have found themselves unresponsive to other mantrams have protested that *Rama* does not mean anything to them either. It may be a while before the mantram "takes," so don't feel disappointed if it doesn't work miracles the first time you repeat it. When you have used the mantram for a while, you'll see for yourself what a difference it can make in your life. People who have begun to use *Rama* on the strength of this advice – experimentally, so to say – usually tell me later, "You know, *Rama* really works."

Another caution which I would sound here is not to use the impersonal mantram *Om* by itself. I sometimes find people who do not respond to any of the mantrams centered around a personal divine figure, such as *Jesus, Jesus.* When such people tell me that they would like to use *Om* as their mantram, I suggest instead that they choose one of the more personal mantrams which begin with *Om*; with such a mantram they are calling on both the personal and impersonal aspects of the supreme reality we call God. There is a good reason for this. People who feel great devotion to a personal incarnation like Jesus the Christ will naturally use his name as their mantram; that very devotion will drive the mantram deeper into their consciousness and release still more devotion. But those who would use an impersonal mantram will find that reaction against childhood associations or intellectual allegiance to the unmanifest Absolute is no substitute for devotion; it will not draw them on. "*Amor saca amor*," Saint Teresa of Avila tells us: love draws out love. There is a deep vein of devotion in all of us if we can only tap it. So even for those who feel little devotion now, sustained use of one of the personal mantrams will bring devotion.

DON'T CHANGE YOUR MANTRAM

No matter what the associations of your past, it is always possible to choose a mantram that can come to appeal to you deeply. Then, once you have chosen your mantram, do not change it. As one of the Desert Fathers, writing on the Prayer of Jesus, warns us with a homely image, a tree that is too often transplanted will not take root. Sri Ramakrishna tells us the same thing when he compares a person who keeps changing mantrams to a farmer who digs in ten different places looking for water. He starts digging for a while in one spot and goes on until the digging gets a little difficult. "The soil is too hard here," he says, and he goes somewhere else where the ground is softer. But soon it starts to cave in around his shovel, and he says, "It is too crumbly here." Then he goes elsewhere and digs until he hits a rock, and so he continues throughout the day. If he could put the same amount of time and energy into digging in one place, he would go deep enough to reach water, and his crops would flourish. It is exactly the same with the mantram. Don't lose heart if after three weeks you don't have spectacular results. It takes time, but once you have made the mantram an integral part of your consciousness, it will bear a rich harvest in joy, security, and a sense of unity with all life.

There have been people who hear my instructions on the mantram and go off full of enthusiasm repeating *Rama, Rama, Rama*. Then they come to me the next day and say, "Perhaps I would have been better off repeating *Jesus, Jesus, Jesus*, but I have been saying *Rama, Rama, Rama* for a whole day now." Let me assure you that using a mantram for one day doesn't commit you to that mantram for life, but within a reasonable period you should settle on the mantram which you feel suits you best. Then, no matter what happens, you will not need to change it again.

A PERSONAL SPIRITUAL IDEAL

It is one of the most penetrating insights into spiritual life to realize that God will guide different people in accordance with their personal needs. In my own ancestral family, which has been religious for many centuries, God is approached as Shiva, for whom my ancestors have built a great temple. Yet I approach God as Sri Krishna. For my grandmother, the spiritual ideal was Sri Rama, and for my mother it was a particular form of Shiva. So philosophically oriented people say, "Your grandmother must have chosen Rama, your mother must have chosen Shiva, and you must have chosen Krishna." I can't say whether my granny chose Rama or Rama chose my granny; I can't say whether my mother chose Shiva or Shiva chose my mother. But I can say for myself, that I did not choose Krishna; Krishna chose me, in his infinite love, in spite of my unworthiness.

This is the realization each of us will have if we repeat the mantram faithfully: God *has* to respond to our earnest call, and he will respond in the way that is best for us. This is the testimony of all the great men and women of God in all the world's spiritual traditions.

Yet the form in which our call is answered is not up to us.

When your meditation has deepened, when your devotion has deepened, and the time comes for you to have a revelation of God, don't have any expectations of how God should reveal his presence. This is left to God's awareness of what your inner needs are. I knew an earnest American spiritual aspirant from Harvard who came to India and meditated under the guidance of an orthodox Hindu teacher in a Hindu ashram. Yet when God appeared to him, he appeared as Jesus the Christ. The man could never get over his amazement. He thought that he had forgotten all about Jesus. So you may be in for a surprise.

Choose a mantram that appeals to you, and leave it to God as to which spiritual ideal is best suited to your deepest needs.

CHAPTER THREE ❧
Some Great Mantrams

GOD HAS BEEN called by many names in different lands and different ages, but by whatever name we call, we are calling on the same divine presence, the same ultimate reality. This is the message declared everywhere by those rare men and women who have had the daring and the resoluteness to give everything to realize the supreme goal of life and to see God in the very depths of their consciousness and simultaneously in all those around them. This experience of the indivisible unity of life is one and the same everywhere, but men and women of God tailor their message to suit the needs and temperament of their time, just as I speak English to my friends in this country and my mother tongue, Malayalam, to my mother. Great figures on the spiritual path, such as Jesus the Christ, Moses, the Compassionate Buddha, or Muhammad, have all given us the same message: "Live only for yourself and you will never grow; live for the welfare of all those around you and you will grow to your full stature." The message is the same; only the idioms differ.

So in each tradition we have a different holy name, a

different mantram, but all are equally valid. Many different languages are spoken in India, and in train stations travelers will hear water venders calling out *vellam* in my old state of Kerala, *tanni* in the neighboring state of Tamil Nadu, *nilu* further north in Andhra, and *pani* in Hindi-speaking areas. Since I come from Kerala, I respond to *vellam*: to me, it sounds the most like water of all these words. But to you who speak English, "water" sounds just right. Whatever the name, it is the same water; it is equally refreshing by any name, and it quenches our thirst just as well.

I have no quarrel with different labels and different approaches to the spiritual life. If the divine presence is Christ to you and you respond deeply to Jesus the Christ, well and good; if you call God Allah or Krishna or the Divine Mother, well and good.

I don't even get agitated when people tell me that they don't believe in God at all. Usually they are thinking of something, or someone, external, some extraterrestrial being swinging between Neptune and Pluto. When I use the word *God*, I am not referring to anything separate from us, but to the divine ground of existence of which we are all part. God is the supreme reality which is the very core of our being, ever pure, ever perfect. He – or she – is our real nature, my real me, your real you. So when people tell me they don't believe in God, I simply ask them, "Do you believe in yourself?" "Of course," they say. "Then," I reply, "you *do* believe in God." Such people still respond to the supreme reality, whether they call it the

Clear Light or collective consciousness or whatever else they prefer.

I had an English friend on the Blue Mountain in South India who used to be allergic to the word *God* or *Lord*; he always spoke of "Nature with a capital *N*." So when he would ask me how my mother's health was, I used to tell him, "She is doing very well, thanks to the grace of Nature with a capital *N*." So no matter what word we use, we are all speaking the same language.

THE PERSONAL GOD

Most mantrams symbolize the personal aspect of God. Although the supreme reality which we call God is present everywhere, throughout the vast cosmos and in the heart of every living creature, he has taken on a human form from age to age so that we might see him and love him and be inspired by his example. Two thousand years ago, in a humble stable in Bethlehem, he came to us as Jesus the Christ and worked for us until his body was crucified. Five hundred years before that he came as the Compassionate Buddha, a prince who turned his back on an earthly throne to walk the dusty roads of ancient India, preaching that our fulfillment lies in extinguishing our self-will and learning to live for the welfare of all. Three thousand years ago he came to us as Krishna to give us the Bhagavad Gita. Each time a divine incarnation comes to us, it is not to bring new truths or to establish a new religion but to remind us of what we have forgotten: that we are all one, and that we must live in harmony with this unity by learning to contribute to the joy and fulfillment of all.

These are personal incarnations of the divine presence that is always within us, but there is also an impersonal form of God, called *Brahman* in Sanskrit. Brahman is not just God; Brahman is the total Godhead, which is beyond thought, which has no attributes, which can't be defined or expressed. So you can't pray to Brahman. You can't ask Brahman to come to your rescue, and you can't really even conceive of Brahman because it has no qualities, no attributes. Only very, very extraordinary people in any religious tradition have realized Brahman – for example, Shankara from my own home state of Kerala and Meister Eckhart of Germany.

When we want a God who has a relationship to us all, who has a relationship to the universe, whom we can love, who will rescue us in times of distress, we want a personal God, a personal manifestation of the attributeless Godhead. There is sound psychology behind this.

THE CHRISTIAN TRADITION

For any Christian, the very name of Jesus is a great mantram, in which we are asking Jesus the Christ to help us to become more like him – full of wisdom, full of mercy, full of love. In my old state of Kerala – where, according to tradition, the Christian community was founded by the apostle Thomas himself – Indian Christians call on the Lord as *Yesu Christu.*

In keeping with their Hindu surroundings, they may even add *Om* and use *Om Yesu Christu* as their mantram. In the Eastern Orthodox tradition, a Christian mantram known as the Prayer of Jesus has long been practiced: *Lord Jesus Christ, Son of God, have mercy on us*. This holy name is sometimes shortened to *Lord Jesus Christ*. The Desert Fathers, holy men living in the deserts of Egypt in the third and fourth centuries, bequeathed us the Prayer of Jesus along with detailed instructions on how to use it, based on their personal experience passed from generation to generation. There is also a marvelous little book called *The Way of a Pilgrim* in which a humble, anonymous villager in Imperial Russia describes in simple and moving words how he came to use the Prayer of Jesus and how it transformed his consciousness.

In the Catholic tradition, *Hail Mary* may be used as a very powerful mantram, full of the infinite love of Mother Mary. In India we say that as long as a child is playing contentedly with its toys beside the back door, the mother keeps busy inside. But eventually the child gets tired of the toys, throws them away, and gives one full-throated cry for its mother. Then she drops everything, rushes to the door, picks up the child tenderly, and comforts it. In just the same way, when you and I stop playing with our toys of pleasure and profit, power and prestige, and call for Mother Mary with all our heart, she will reveal herself to us in the depths of our consciousness.

A RUSSIAN MANTRAM

The treasure of world mysticism mentioned above, *The Way of a Pilgrim*, is the story of an anonymous Russian pilgrim of the nineteenth century whose primary spiritual practice was repeating the Russian version of the Jesus Prayer: *Gospodi pomilui,* "Lord, have mercy." It kept him company through many adventures as he wandered along the roads of the vast land of Russia. Though possessing little more than the clothes he wore, and often facing real hardship, he says,

> The prayer of the heart gave me such consolation that
> I felt there was no happier person on earth than I, and
> I doubted if there could be greater and fuller happiness
> in the kingdom of heaven. Not only did I feel this in
> my own soul, but the whole outside world also seemed
> to me full of charm and delight.

A GREEK MANTRAM

The Prayer of Jesus is also used in the Greek Orthodox tradition. The full form of this prayer, used by the monks of Mount Athos, is *Kyrie emon, Yesou Christe, Yie Theou, eleison emas:* "Lord Jesus Christ, Son of God, have mercy on us."

Repetition of the Jesus Prayer has been an important spiritual exercise in the Eastern Orthodox church for centuries. Saint John of the Ladder, from this tradition, says,

> Prayer by reason of its nature is the converse and
> union of man with God, and by reason of its action

upholds the world and brings about reconciliation
with God; it is the mother and also the daughter of
tears, the propitiation for sins, a bridge over tempta-
tions, a wall against afflictions, a crushing of conflicts,
work of angels, food of all spiritual beings, future
gladness, boundless activity, the spring of virtues, the
source of graces, invisible progress, food of the soul,
the enlightening of the mind, an axe for despair, a
demonstration of hope, the annulling of sorrow, the
wealth of monks, the treasure of solitaries, the reduc-
tion of anger, the mirror of progress, the realization of
success, the proof of one's condition, a revelation of the
future, and a sign of glory.

RAMA

In Indian mysticism we refer to a divine incarnation as an
avatara or *avatar: ava* means "down"; *tri,* "to cross or come."
Avatara is "one who comes down" – the supreme reality whom
we call God appearing on the face of the earth as a human
being like us in response to the tremendous needs of the
world, in response to people who are in dire distress. It's a
magnificent concept. In India, we have many incarnations of
God, and that explains the hospitality of the Hindu heart to
all religions and to all spiritual teachers. But among the many
forms of God, among the many mantrams used in India, I'd
like to present Rama and Krishna first. These are universal figures, and they appeal to everyone.

In the Hindu tradition, *Rama* is one of the simplest, most powerful, and most popular of mantrams. This holy name comes from the Sanskrit root *ram,* "to rejoice"; *Rama* means "he who fills us with abiding joy." When we repeat this mantram, we are reminding ourselves of the source of abiding joy deep within us. It was through the ceaseless repetition of *Rama, Rama, Rama* that the very ordinary young man Mohandas Karamchand Gandhi transformed himself into Mahatma Gandhi, who freed India from the greatest empire the world has ever seen without firing a single shot.

Rama is one of the most popular mantrams in India, and the *Ramayana,* which tells Prince Rama's story, is the most popular and beloved epic in all India. For many reasons it is very easy to identify with Rama. Rama undergoes much suffering, has his heart broken many times. He is trapped in many terrible situations. If you ask our sages, "Why does God suffer? How would God ever be caught in these terrible situations?" our sages will say with great devotion, "That's how God becomes accessible and easy for us to identify with." In Western mysticism, there is a similar saying that God incarnates as a human being so that humans can be lifted to become divine. "He became man that we might be made God," said Saint Athanasius. Though Rama undergoes many trials, he is always the ideal son, brother, husband, king. He is an ideal, and yet he is one of us.

In our early days as children in India, when we hear the story of the *Ramayana* from our parents or grandparents, it's not the story of God that we listen to. It is not the story of an extraordinary leader. It's our own story. If you look at the opening of the *Ramayana*, you will see conflicts just like the ones that rage today within families and races and nations. Rama does not live in a trouble-free world, but he overcomes the terrible challenges that stand in the way of the fulfillment of his destiny. Exiled, attacked, suffering the loss of his beloved wife, Sita, and then waging a successful battle against the forces of evil, Rama eventually attains his rightful place as ruler of his kingdom.

This is spiritual allegory of a high order, but it is not necessary for us to understand all the rich lore of the Rama legend to use the *Rama* mantram. It is enough to understand that *Rama* means joy and stands for spiritual enlightenment in a world of trial, where good finally triumphs over evil and joy over suffering. "The rule of Rama" is a phrase that Gandhi took from the Hindu scriptures, and it refers to a kingdom in which the love we have for one another is never diminished, a kingdom ruled by justice, not violence. When we repeat the mantram *Rama, Rama, Rama,* we are asking that this kingdom of heaven be established here on earth.

When we use the *Rama* mantram, we are not calling on the Rama whose story is told in legend but the Rama who lives within us as our truest Self, here and now.

Rama is at the heart of many other powerful mantrams in India. One is the mantram of Swami Ramdas, *Om Sri Ram jai Ram jai jai Ram,* which I heard being chanted when my wife and I visited his spiritual community in South India many years ago. In practical language, this mantram means simply,

"May joy prevail." With the repetition of this mantram, we are praying that the abiding joy in the depths of our consciousness prevail over all that is selfish in us and bring us the joy that comes with realizing the indivisible unity of life.

KRISHNA

Another incarnation with universal appeal is Krishna, whose name means "he who draws us to himself." In traditional Hindu language, the Godhead has three functions: creation, preservation, and destruction. Krishna is the full form of God as the preserver or savior of the universe.

Just as the *Ramayana* tells the story of Rama, the *Mahabharata* is the epic which tells the story of Krishna and how he acts as the guide and teacher of the forces of light in their struggle with the forces of evil. One of the world's best-loved scriptures, the Bhagavad Gita, is a part of the *Mahabharata*, and it contains the essence of Krishna's teachings. I would recommend it to anyone interested in exploring the richness of this tradition.

There is a vast literature surrounding the avatar of Krishna. Most of the episodes from this classic Hindu tradition are simple reminders that behind the charming figure of Krishna, the gentle teacher, is the infinite, eternal power that preserves and protects the entire cosmos. This is the power that the mantram *Krishna* calls upon.

It is not important or necessary to become acquainted with the spiritual allegory of Krishna in great detail. What is important is to remember that when we use this mantram we are calling on the Krishna who symbolizes the Self within us, the Lord of Love.

One of the best-loved mantrams in India, and one that is well known in the West too, combines three beautiful names of the Lord:

> *Hare Rama Hare Rama,*
> *Rama Rama Hare Hare,*
> *Hare Krishna Hare Krishna,*
> *Krishna Krishna Hare Hare.*

The third name here, *Hare,* is the vocative form of *Hari,* "he who steals our hearts." When the Lord sent us into this world, he stole our heart and then looked about for a suitable place to hide with it. "If I hide on the highest mountain," he said, "people will climb it and find me. If I hide in the atom, they will split it and find me. If I hide in the stars, they will spy me out with their telescopes." So the Lord hid in the last place we would ever look – in the depths of our own consciousness. We all hear his call, we are all looking for him, but most of us don't know where to look. We go to Reno thinking he might be there; we look in the kitchen, in the bar, in the library, in the bank, in our music collection. But the Lord has stolen our heart, and we will never find lasting fulfillment in any of these places; we will find what we are really looking for only in the depths of our own consciousness, in the kingdom of heaven within.

If you choose to use *Hare Rama, Hare Krishna* as given above, you can use *Rama* as the short form of your mantram.

This is not the same as changing your mantram or using two different mantrams. It is helpful to use *Rama* when you need a short, powerful word – for example, when the mind is agitated. At other times, you may use the longer form of the mantram. My granny used the longer form while sweeping the veranda in the calm morning hour, but when I needed a mantram to rescue me from my fears, she suggested that I use *Rama, Rama, Rama* .

SHIVA

Om namah Shivaya, a mantram that is especially popular in South India, is a supplication to the Lord as Shiva. In the Hindu Trinity, in which the principles of creation, preservation, and destruction are personified, Shiva is the destructive aspect of the Godhead, and in this mantram we are calling upon him to put an end to our selfishness, to our sense of separateness. This mantram reminds us that the Lord has a sterner side. He loves us all with infinite tenderness, but he is also prepared to make us suffer a little if suffering will teach us to make the wise choices in life which enable us to grow to our full stature.

It is one of the most bitter truths in life that pain often goes hand in hand with growth. On the physical level, for example, poor eating habits and too little exercise lead to all sorts of physical problems. If the resulting pain spurs us to change our way of living, then pain has helped us to grow. On the spiritual level, when we live selfishly, basing our lives on the pursuit of our own private satisfactions, we suffer alienation from those around us. The nagging suspicion that we have not found real fulfillment will not give us any peace. If it enables us to change our ways and learn to live for the welfare of those around us, then this suffering is a sign of grace.

BUDDHIST MANTRAMS

In Japan, the traditional Buddhist mantram comes directly from Sanskrit: *Namu Amidabutsu,* "I put my faith in the Buddha of infinite light." But the oldest mantram in Buddhism, revered everywhere, is *Om mani padme hum,* which refers to the "jewel in the lotus of the heart." This jewel is the permanent treasure of joy and security hidden deep within us, waiting to be discovered. Here the heart is compared to a lotus, which is one of the most beloved of spiritual symbols in Hinduism and Buddhism. In the village in Kerala state in which I grew up, there were two beautiful lotus ponds. The lotus would grow up from the muddy bottoms of these ponds, but the mud would not stain its lovely, waxen petals. For this reason, the lotus is a perfect symbol of purity, reminding us that whatever mistakes we may have committed in the past, we can all purify our consciousness through systematic repetition of the mantram; our hearts can open with love and compassion for all.

Twenty-five hundred years ago, men and women from all over India, and later from all over Asia, were drawn to the Compassionate Buddha to learn the supreme art of living from him. There are many significant stories that have come down to us that give a clear picture of the greatness of the Buddha as a spiritual teacher. Perhaps the single quality about him that appeals most deeply to the modern spirit is his unflinching search for truth, his refusal to believe any dogma that has not been verified in personal experience.

There is one story in particular that demonstrates the Buddha's insistence on personal realization. It is about a very argumentative student of the Buddha. Any professor will be able to tell you about such people. They are usually not welcome additions to the classroom, but the Buddha, being the Compassionate One, had a soft corner in his heart for this student, whose name was Malunkyaputra. He used to ask the Compassionate Buddha, "What is nirvana? When you attain nirvana, what happens to the body? When you attain nirvana, what continues afterwards as your personality?" When he went on asking these questions, the Buddha never lost his patience, but finally told Malunkyaputra a story about a man wounded on the battlefield by a poisoned arrow. When the surgeon came to operate, the wounded man said, "Before you remove the arrow, tell me who shot it. Was he from Punjab or Kerala? Was he tall or short? What kind of bow did he use?" The Buddha said, "Malunkyaputra, it is possible for all these questions to be answered, but by the time they are answered, the wounded person will have died." Malunkyaputra finally got the point.

The Buddha carefully avoided impractical questions. It saved him a lot of energy. He replied to impractical, speculative questions with a noble silence. There is not enough time in life to satisfy all of our curiosity, even curiosity about spiritual matters. There is only enough time to practice spiritual disciplines and realize spiritual truths for ourselves. That is what the mantram *Om mani padme hum* stands for: personal realization of the jewel that lies in the heart of each of us.

JEWISH MANTRAMS

In the Jewish tradition, *Barukh attah Adonai* means "Blessed art thou, O Lord." The Lord is the source of all strength, all courage, all joy, all love, and the greatest blessing we can know is to realize him in the depths of our consciousness and gain access to these deeper resources, which the Lord will magnify in us for his service. Another Hebrew mantram, used by Hasidic Jews, is *Ribono shel olam,* "Lord of the universe." The whole of creation is his; our lives rest in his hands. With the mantram we can learn to shift the burden of all our personal problems onto the Lord, releasing the resources we need to deal with them.

A little story from the Hasidic tradition reminds us that we can remember God always by repeating the holy name. In this story a man asks his *zaddik,* his spiritual teacher, "Do you mean we should remember the Lord even in the give-and-take of business?" "Yes, of course," the rabbi replies. "If you can remember business matters in the hour of prayer, shouldn't you try to remember God in the transactions of your business?"

The Jewish tradition is rich in beautiful stories and verses that remind us of the sweetness of repeating the holy name, for as it says in the Book of Isaiah, "The desire of our soul is to thy name, and to the remembrance of thee."

MUSLIM MANTRAMS

Bismillah ir-Rahman ir-Rahim is a beautiful Muslim mantram, meaning "In the name of Allah, the merciful, the compassionate." The Lord, who is the source of all mercy and compassion, has given us a wide margin to experiment with the playthings of life. Once we set our hearts on becoming united with him, the burden of past mistakes will fall away. Orthodox Muslims say this mantram before they speak, as a reminder that everything we say and do should be in accord with the will of God, the indivisible unity of life.

The name *Allah* itself, or *Allahu akbar*, "God is great," are also Muslim mantrams. In the annals of Islamic mysticism we find a precise exposition of the power of the holy name to transform us:

> All the hundred and twenty-four thousand prophets
> were sent to preach one word. They bade the people
> say *Allah* and devote themselves to him. Those who
> heard this word by the ear alone let it go out by the
> other ear; but those who heard it with their souls imprinted it on their souls and repeated it until it penetrated their hearts and souls, and their whole being
> became this word. They were made independent of the
> pronunciation of the word; they were released from
> the sound of the letters. Having understood the spiri-

tual meaning of this word, they became so absorbed in it that they were no more conscious of their separate selves.

Each one of us can become so absorbed in the mantram that we are no longer preoccupied with ourselves. When we have become aware of the unity of life, we will find our joy in contributing to the joy of those around us; we will find our fulfillment in helping those around us to grow.

THE IMPERSONAL

These are all mantrams which call upon the personal aspect of God. But God has an impersonal aspect as well, which a few mantrams reflect. This impersonal aspect has been called by many formidable-sounding names: the Unmanifested, the transcendental Godhead, the ultimate reality, the Absolute, Brahman. All these names are inadequate, because the underlying reality of existence is beyond name and form, beyond time and space, beyond cause and effect. Jesus taught us to pray to our Father in heaven, Sri Ramakrishna in nineteenth-century Bengal worshipped the Divine Mother, and Sufi mystics in the Islamic tradition call upon the Beloved, but there were sages in ancient India who did not refer to God as either *he* or *she*; for them the ultimate reality was *it* or *that*.

The perfect symbol of the impersonal aspect of the Godhead is the syllable *Om*. In Hinduism and Buddhism, many mantrams based on the personal aspect of the Lord begin with *Om,* so that a single mantram symbolizes the divine presence as both personal and impersonal, manifest and unmanifest.

To explain why *Om* is such a perfect symbol of the impersonal Godhead, it is necessary to refer to a theory in the ancient Hindu scriptures which has much in common with recent discoveries in modern science. According to this theory, the entire phenomenal world consists of vibrations, just as matter, according to modern physics, may be looked at as a concentration of energy. The physicist will tell you that in the last analysis, this book is not a solid object; it is a structure of vibrating energies temporarily fixed in a particular pattern. In the Hindu theory of vibration, matter is the most rigid, the most "condensed" of vibrations; it is solid and perceptible to the senses. Energy is less rigid, more subtle. It is not solid and often not perceptible, but it is not different in kind from matter; it is still patterns of vibration, only in a more subtle state. The subtlest of vibrations, according to the ancient sages, is the so-called cosmic sound, the creative Word out of which the entire universe of stars and seas, plants and animals and human beings has evolved. The passage from Saint John – "In the beginning was the Word, and the Word was with God, and the Word was God" – has an almost exact parallel in the Rig Veda, one of the oldest of Hindu scriptures, which speaks of the unmanifested Godhead, called Brahman: "In the beginning was Brahman, with whom was the Word, and the Word was truly the supreme Brahman."

This Word, the cosmic sound, is not perceptible to the senses, but it can be experienced in very deep meditation. It is most closely approximated by the syllable *Om* – or *Aum,* as it is sometimes pronounced. When we utter *Om* with awareness of its significance, we are to some degree evoking the supreme reality for which it stands.

Once a man and woman who had been meditating under my guidance for a short while came to me and said that they had been hearing the cosmic sound. Their meditation was not likely to have been so very deep, so to get to the root of the matter I went to their home one morning to meditate with them. It turned out that they had been hearing the hum of the refrigerator. The real experience of the cosmic sound, as attested by mystics from the East and West alike, is something profound. Saint Francis of Assisi, for example, described it as a music so sweet and so beautiful that had it lasted a moment longer, he would have melted away from the sheer joy of it.

In any case, whether you accept the theory of vibration or not, *Om* is still a magnificent symbol. For thousands of years it has stood for the ultimate reality – the transcendental Godhead beyond all names and forms, beyond all sects and all denominations.

Most of us, however, do not respond deeply to the impersonal aspect of the ultimate reality. I sometimes tease my friends by asking them how they would like to have an impersonal girlfriend, a transcendental boyfriend. She is unmanifested, so how can you gaze into her eyes? He is beyond time and space, so how can you hold his hand? What most of us need and want is a personal incarnation: a figure whom we can visualize, whom we can hear stories about, whom we can love and try to model ourselves after, whether we call him Christ, Krishna, or the Buddha, or her the Divine Mother.

So most of the great mantrams of the world's religions center around these tremendous figures. Such mantrams help us to cultivate an ever-deepening devotion, and can assist us in becoming united with the divine presence in the depths of our consciousness.

THE NAMES OF GOD ARE INFINITE

These are some of the most widely used and best-loved mantrams in the great religious traditions of the world, but there are many other names too by which men and women through the ages have called on God for strength and support. Saint Francis of Assisi repeated "My God and my all" to help transform himself from Francis the would-be troubadour into Francis the instrument of God's love. And in the Hindu tradition, there are magnificent hymns called *The Thousand Names of the Lord* and *The Thousand Names of the Divine Mother* which give us a vast selection of beautiful holy names. But many mantrams, especially in Hinduism or Buddhism, come out of a complex tradition whose references may be too elusive for us. Such mantrams are not likely to evoke a deep response in those who were not brought up in these traditions. So I stress those mantrams which are short, simple, and powerful, which come out of a long, established tradition and have carried many devoted men and women safely across the tempestuous sea of life.

CHAPTER FOUR

Making the Mantram a Part of Your Day

YOU DON'T HAVE to have set times to repeat the mantram; you can repeat it whenever you get a chance. When you begin to look for opportunities to say the mantram, you find them everywhere. If you get five minutes at the post office, that is five minutes that you can use for repeating *Rama, Rama, Rama* or *Jesus, Jesus, Jesus.* Later, while waiting for the bus, you get five minutes more – or ten minutes, or maybe even twenty. This is how you get time to say the holy name, by becoming like a miser with all the little moments you get throughout the day. You don't have to wait for a stretch of two hours when no one is going to disturb you; it will never happen. Every day you pick up a few minutes here and a few minutes there. And by the end of the year, you have a high investment. It all adds up, as the bank advertisements say.

WHILE WAITING

The little waits and delays that life is so full of are all opportunities to use the mantram. In the morning when you're waiting for the coffee to brew, you can repeat the mantram instead of staring blankly at the wall. When you are standing in line at the bank, or the post office, or the supermarket, the mantram will make the wait seem shorter, and your example of calm and patience will help those around you too. When you are waiting for an interview or for a test to begin or for the doctor to come in, the mantram can save you a good deal of anxiety, which will lower your blood pressure and improve your performance. In all these cases you are putting your time to better use than if you were just letting your mind run on about what is troubling it.

WHILE WALKING

Walking is one of the best times to repeat the mantram, especially if you walk briskly. The rhythm of your footsteps, the rhythm of the mantram, and the rhythm of your breathing all harmonize to soothe and invigorate the body and mind. This happens naturally, and there is nothing mysterious about it. Breathing is closely connected with our state of mind. People who are tense or angry breathe rapidly and irregularly; those who are calm, loving, and secure breathe like a little child, smoothly, slowly, and deeply. A brisk walk helps to make your breathing rhythm deep and even, and the mantram will help to calm your mind. So at work, try a mantram break: take a brisk five- or ten-minute walk repeating the mantram and see how much better you feel than if you had stayed at your desk with a cup of coffee. The mantram goes well with other rhythmical forms of exercise too, like jogging, swimming, or bicycle riding, but I especially recommend walking because it requires no special equipment and no special time, and you can keep it up right into the evening of your life.

A PART OF THE DAILY ROUTINE

You can make the mantram part of your daily routine in many other ways, too. For example, if you spend a lot of time reading or writing or typing, it is good to rest your eyes from time to time by looking up from your work and gazing into the distance. This is a perfect chance to use the mantram, and for people who are driven by their work, it is also a good exercise in detachment. If you find yourself working compulsively, just see how hard it is to drop your work for one minute to give your full attention to the mantram.

My friends and I shut our eyes and repeat the mantram silently for a moment before each meal. This reminds us that the food we are about to eat is a gift, and that the energy it gives us should be used in the service of others. This is especially helpful at lunch for people who are at work, away from the supporting circle of family and friends; at least once during the busy workday it is helpful to stop and remember the divine presence within. If you are feeling tense and harried, with your stomach in knots and the gastric juices at war with one another, the mantram says, "All right, boys, break it up!" After all, mealtime is not the time to get involved in heated discussions or critical talk. A nourishing meal, cooked and served with love and eaten in the cheerful company of family or friends, is a sacrament, and the mantram is a beautiful way to begin it.

WHEN SICK

When you are sick or suffering any physical discomfort, the mantram is of great value. As more attention goes to the mantram, there is less attention for the physical sensations of discomfort or pain.

Even seasickness is susceptible to this. When I was coming to this country by ship, we ran into a storm in the Indian Ocean which lasted for days. I had never been at sea before, and I must say that even blueberry waffles lose their appeal when you're looking down into the sea one instant and staring up at the sky the next. One by one, even the most seasoned of my fellow passengers took quietly to the rails. But I just took to my mantram. One morning, towards the end of the storm, I walked into the dining hall for breakfast and found myself entirely alone in that vast room. I was able to do justice to a hearty breakfast, too. This impressed not only my fellow passengers but the crew also, and they were all asking me what kind of tablet I took. So when you have a headache or a toothache or any of the hundred and one other afflictions that can come our way, take an aspirin if you like, but be sure to say the mantram.

If you are really ill, instead of lying in bed watching television or solving crossword puzzles or just staring at the cracks in the ceiling, you can put this time to much better use by repeating the mantram. It will not only comfort you and take your mind off the pain; it can release curative forces from deep within. There is nothing occult about this. A good deal of the suffering involved in illness comes from dwelling on the symptoms, from worrying about how serious the illness is and when you will recover and how you will manage to carry on. This anxiety impedes your recovery, and you can use the mantram to keep such worries from clouding your mind. In a mind that is at ease, the positive power of the mantram cannot help releasing the deep curative forces that are the body's natural and most effective measures for restoring health.

WHILE DOING MECHANICAL TASKS

The mantram goes well with any mechanical task that doesn't demand your full attention, especially if the task is rhythmic. You can repeat the mantram in your mind while washing dishes or polishing your shoes, while sweeping or sawing, even while you are brushing your teeth. All too often, when we are engaged in mechanical tasks of this sort, the better part of our attention is far from the job at hand. We may be daydreaming or woolgathering – thinking about yesterday, rehearsing what we would like to say to our boss if we ever get the chance, letting some old song run through our mind, dwelling on a pet worry or resentment. Much more of our vitality than we suspect ebbs out through this constant play of the mind. We are deluding ourselves if we think that our minds are always gainfully occupied, moving with clear logical precision from premise to conclusion. When we repeat the mantram while doing mechanical jobs, we are not only sending the mantram deeper into our consciousness; we are training our minds to stay in the here and now.

WHEN NOT TO SAY THE MANTRAM

Let me also add a word of caution about when *not* to say the mantram. Some people can get so enthusiastic about the mantram that they get carried away and repeat it when they should be devoting their full attention to what they are doing. Do not try to repeat the mantram when you are engaged in conversation, listening to instructions, reading or writing, or listening to good music. Also, do not repeat it when you are working at a potentially dangerous job – say, one involving sharp tools or powerful machinery, whether it is a big electric saw or just sharp knives in the kitchen. That is the time to give your complete attention to the job at hand. For the same reason, I do not recommend repeating the mantram while driving, especially in heavy traffic, because of the danger of getting absorbed in the mantram and not paying enough attention to the wheel, to your speed, to other cars, and to pedestrians and animals. Beyond this, it is up to each individual to decide what jobs are worthy of his or her full attention. A skilled carpenter may be able to say the mantram each time he swings his hammer. That is fine for him, but if I tried it, I have very little doubt that I would hit my thumb. So use your own judgment here.

BOREDOM

The mantram can also be of great help when you have time on your hands. Boredom can be a real source of problems to people who don't know what to do with their time and attention. My wife and I used to walk around Lake Merritt in Oakland every morning, and I was always fascinated by the ways in which commuters would spend their ten or fifteen minutes while waiting for a bus to San Francisco. Many of them were smoking, not because they especially wanted to but because they didn't know what else to do with their time; and one chap, dressed to take on the bulls and bears on Montgomery Street, seemed intent on trying to drill a hole in the Oakland sidewalk with his umbrella. All of these people could have benefited greatly from the mantram. Most of us, in fact, do not realize how much of what we do is motivated simply by boredom, by restlessness, by not knowing what to do with our time. Here the mantram can save us a good deal of agitation and wasted energy, which we often court when we are bored by letting our minds run away with us.

Indiscriminate television watching is one sure sign of boredom. Friends of mine who work in hospitals tell me that many patients have the television going all day long, sometimes even with two sets both on in a single room, just because they do not know what else to do with their time. I would say, turn off the television, lie back, and repeat the mantram; the silence and the mantram will speed your recovery much more than a soap opera. I am particularly grieved when I hear of elderly people in retirement homes and convalescent hospitals parked in their wheelchairs in front of a blaring television set. I think, if only they had the mantram, what a good companion it would be for them. My mother, who lived with me in her last years, devoted hours each day to the mantram. If she had been asked – and if she could have spoken English – she would have told you without hesitation that she didn't know the meaning of boredom.

For younger people who are active and healthy, of course, I am not suggesting nonstop repetition of the mantram in place of all the hours they now spend watching television. A grim statistic says that our children spend an average of over six hours a day in front of a television set, and adults are not far behind. When there is a good show, educational or wholesomely entertaining, let us watch, by all means, but otherwise we could invest these hours much more profitably. There are so many worthwhile activities that everyone in the family can participate in. We can walk or go swimming together; we can rediscover the lost art of conversation, getting to know our family and our friends and our neighbors better; we can devote a portion of our time to selfless causes which contribute to the welfare of all.

LITTLE COMPULSIONS

Then there are people who must always be reading something. At breakfast they read and reread what is written on the milk carton; on the bus going to work they pull out a novel or a crossword puzzle; when they go to clean the attic, they get caught by the old magazines piled in the corner. Wouldn't it be better to repeat the mantram than to go on reading everything in sight, just because it is there?

People who are compulsive talkers are not too different. There is a Sufi proverb that each word we utter should have to pass through three gates before we say it. At the first gate, the gatekeeper asks, "Is this true?" At the second gate, he asks, "Is it kind?" And at the third gate, "Is it necessary?" If we applied this proverb strictly, most of us would have very little to say. I am not recommending silence, however, but control over our speech.

Talk is good when it communicates, and cheerful, positive speech in moderation helps to maintain relations between family and friends. But those who are compulsive talkers can turn it to their advantage by repeating the mantram, and they can go a long way. Today it may be "Blah, blah, blah," but when the mantram finally takes hold, it will be "Rama, Rama, Rama." This is the way liabilities are turned into assets on the spiritual path.

WHILE GOING TO SLEEP

One of the most important times to use the mantram is at night, when you are going to sleep. This is the time when all our problems come home to roost – all the turmoil of the day, all the anxieties of the following morning. This is why we have bad dreams, why we don't sleep very well and get up wishing we could sleep four hours more. So instead of falling asleep in your problems, put your book away, turn out the light, close your eyes, and begin repeating *Rama, Rama, Rama* or *Jesus, Jesus, Jesus* until you fall asleep in it. It takes some time and some effort to master this, but once you are able to fall asleep in the mantram, it will go on working its healing effect in your consciousness throughout the night.

Between the last waking moment and the first sleeping moment, there is an arrow's entry into the depths of your consciousness. This is one of the great discoveries in the unification of consciousness. It is a marvelous moment. You are neither awake nor asleep; you are between two worlds, and the tunnel is open. At that moment, you can send the mantram in just the way a bowler bowls a strike. You have seen how a good bowler picks up the ball and cradles it in his free hand, aims, and sends the ball rolling down the lane with just the right degree of spin to score a strike. It's very much like that with the mantram; you can learn to send the mantram right into the depths of your mind every night.

When this happens, you may hear the mantram in your dreams, reverberating in the depths of your consciousness. It is an exceedingly rewarding experience, and one which will protect you in your sleep. A friend once told me that he had long been subject to a certain recurrent nightmare, but one night, just as this nightmare was working up to its usual fearful climax, he heard the mantram echoing in his consciousness. It dispelled the fear and the bad dream, too, and that nightmare has never been back to haunt him again. So when you have learned to fall asleep in the mantram, it is goodbye to nightmares, to disquieting dreams, to that feeling that the night hasn't exactly been refreshing.

As you are learning to fall asleep in the mantram, you are likely to be paying more attention than before to the process of falling asleep, and you may observe things which you have never noticed before. The body may give a sudden twitch, or you may hear little voices or even see things. There is nothing occult about this, and nothing to be alarmed at. If such experiences occur while you are falling asleep, pay no attention to them; just hang on to the mantram. Scientists call this twilight zone between waking and sleeping the hypnogogic state; I like to call it Alice's Wonderland. Before we are actually asleep, the conscious mind is closing up shop and the trap door to the subconscious may open a crack to let a few stray wisps of consciousness waft out. Pay no attention to them. They are not angelic voices, and they are not clues to the innermost workings of your mind; they have no more significance than the ever-changing shapes you can see in clouds drifting by. Quite possibly this sort of thing has always happened as you fell asleep, only you were not aware enough to notice. So when you are making an effort to fall asleep in the mantram, just go on repeating it if these wisps of consciousness come your way.

Falling asleep in the mantram is not as easy as it sounds. It takes some practice, but it is well worth the effort. So if you take a nap during the day, or doze off while riding in a car or bus or plane, or wake up in the middle of the night, just treat these events as opportunities for learning to fall asleep in the mantram. This is especially helpful for those who are subject to bouts of sleeplessness. Instead of lying there watching the clock, getting anxious about how much sleep you're missing or how you will feel in the morning, repeat the mantram. Then instead of complaining, "I missed two hours and forty-three minutes of sleep last night," you can say, "I had two hours and forty-three minutes of uninterrupted time for the mantram." With this change of perspective, and with the mantram soothing your mind, you may soon find yourself a complete stranger to insomnia. And of course in the morning there is nothing like the mantram for beginning the day. When your alarm goes off, you don't have to pull the covers over your head and lie there groaning; the mantram will enable you to fling off your covers and face the challenges of the day with enthusiasm.

WITH CHILDREN

Parents of small children will find the mantram a perfect lullaby. This is especially the case with infants, who may need a lot of attention during the night – a lot of walking, a lot of rocking, a lot of physical contact, all of which may take up several hours. On such occasions, the mantram will not only soothe your baby but also give you the patience you need to get through the night, and it is so restful on a deeper level of consciousness that it can make up a great deal for the sleep you lose.

Sing the mantram to your children; give the mantram to your children when they have to go to the dentist, or when they have to go for an injection. At these times, all children get afraid, and they will welcome the mantram. Let them see you using the mantram, too, on these occasions, and they will observe how it helps you.

When you use the mantram in this way, you are planting it deep in your child's consciousness, which will be an invaluable service to him or her in later years. Mahatma Gandhi absorbed his mantram, *Rama,* in this way, at his nurse's knee, just as I absorbed the *Hare Rama* mantram from hearing it on my granny's lips when I was a young child.

WRITING THE MANTRAM

Writing the mantram is a valuable discipline. In our home we have a big, thick album in which anybody who has a few minutes can sit down and write the mantram. This has quite practical uses. When you are too upset to repeat the mantram calmly in your mind, you will find that you can write it, and that the act of writing will keep your mind from wandering away to whatever is troubling you.

In your home, keep a notebook for writing the mantram. If somebody who is agitated comes to visit you, wanting to discuss their agitation with you and weigh the pros and cons of what action he should take or not take – which is going to agitate you, agitate him, and agitate all connected with you – my suggestion is to give him the mantram album and say, "Why don't you just write *Rama, Rama, Rama* a thousand times?" You will be helping him to calm his mind, and when his mind is calmer, he will be able to solve the problem that is agitating him.

CHANTING THE MANTRAM

By and large, I recommend repeating the mantram silently in the mind. However, there are occasions when chanting it may be of great help. For example, if the mind is in tremendous turmoil and you simply cannot stay with the mantram, go out for a walk where you can be alone, and as you walk briskly, repeat the mantram aloud. I wouldn't do this around others – you may attract unwanted attention – but while alone it can be of great benefit in calming an agitated mind.

If someone in the family is ill, and if all the family and friends share the mantram, getting together to chant can be of great solace to both the family and the person who is ill. This practice of chanting comes right out of our Indian tradition, and I would recommend it for these special occasions. During times of distress, when the mind faces tragedy and resists being brought back into a state of peace and control, a group of sincere spiritual aspirants gathering together to chant the mantram can be of immense help. But don't introduce the mantram into a situation where people are not prepared for it.

PRAYER

When we repeat the mantram, we are calling on God. The mantram is really one of the best of prayers – one that we say not just when we get up or when we go to bed, but countless times throughout the day and throughout the night as well. This prayer is not addressed to anyone or any power outside us, but to our deepest Self, the Lord of Love, who dwells in the hearts of us all. When we repeat the mantram, we are not asking for anything in particular, like good health or solutions to our problems or richer personal relationships. We are simply asking to get closer to the source of all strength and all joy and all love. But as Jesus tells us, "Seek ye first the kingdom of heaven, and all else shall be added unto you." When we ask simply to get closer to the divine presence, we find at the same time that our health improves, our problems begin to be resolved, and all our relationships grow richer and more fulfilling.

CHAPTER FIVE

Keeping the Mind Steady

THE POPULAR ETYMOLOGY of the word *mantram*
gives us some clue what it means to have the holy name at
work in our consciousness. It is said that *mantram* comes
from the roots *man,* "the mind," and *tri,* "to cross." The mantram is that which enables us to cross the sea of the mind. The
sea is a perfect symbol for the mind. It is in constant motion;
there is calm one day and storm the next. We see only the surface, with hardly any inkling of the strange creatures that lurk
below or the tremendous currents that sweep through the
depths. From where we stand on this shore, the far shore is so
completely out of sight that we find it hard even to imagine
that there *is* another shore.

Most of us are aware of the motion of the mind only on the
surface level of consciousness, where our thoughts jump like
grasshoppers from one thing to another. Stray observations
on our surroundings, old memories, plans for the future, a
rush of elation over some good news, regrets over the past, a
line from a popular song, worries about our problems, physical sensations, resentments towards those around us, and a

craving for something to eat all follow one another in just a matter of minutes. In themselves, most of these thoughts are not actually harmful; a few of them may even be rather elevating. The trouble is that we have very little control over them. If you ask the thoughts, they would say, "This poor fellow thinks he is thinking us, but we are thinking *him*."

BELOW THE SURFACE OF CONSCIOUSNESS

Below the surface level of consciousness, what storms rage! Here are our deep-seated fears and hostilities, our cravings and conflicts. These are the deep divisions in our consciousness which make it difficult for us to concentrate, difficult to be loyal and steadfast. Often these divisions are at the root of serious physical ailments. They come to us in our sleep as nightmares, and all too often they plunge us into depression. Such storms sap our will and our vitality.

The vast majority of us see no way to change this situation; we have come to accept it as inevitable, as part of human nature. But let me assure you that this is not our real nature; it is only our conditioning. Deep within us we have immense reserves of will, loyalty, patience, compassion, and love; it is only that we do not know how to unlock these resources and bring them into full play in our daily lives. But this is something all of us can learn to do if we can gain control of our minds.

THE WELL-TRAINED MIND

Control of the mind is something that has never occurred to most of us; to some it may even sound cold or rigid. Many people, especially those who are highly educated, feel that control would stifle the untrammeled freedom of their thoughts. But none of us question the need for control, for discipline, in mastering physical skills. Take eating, for example; it never even occurs to us what dexterity it requires simply to get food onto a fork and guide it to our mouths. Only when we see a baby learning to feed itself, getting more cereal on its face than in its mouth, do we realize that our effortless skill in eating comes from long years of practice. We have taught our hand to obey us. How would you feel if your hand suddenly refused to take orders from you, if it poured the coffee over your salad or fed you soup with the spoon upside down? This is exactly how we let our mind treat us, because we have never given it the proper training. When we want to concentrate, the mind generates a host of irrelevant worries and distractions. When we want to be dedicated, it brings in all sorts of conflicts and reservations. When we want to be loving, it drags out its little collection of trivial resentments and old hostilities. But when we learn to control the mind – to slow down its feverish pace, to welcome those thoughts we approve of and dismiss those that are negative – we will find what a sense of mastery this brings.

When most of us think of self-control, we think of something external. We may manage to keep from doing the wrong thing, but our mind is in turmoil; we may manage to keep from saying the wrong thing, but the words we're thinking are far from parliamentary. Here it is not enough to tell ourselves, "Keep a stiff upper lip, old boy," and put on a calm front. We can all have such control over the mind that calmness becomes our natural state. We can learn to turn our backs on our private satisfactions when necessary without a ripple of protest in the mind, and we can learn to function in the most trying circumstances without a trace of agitation. This is not control imposed from without; it is real mastery over our life.

THE BARRIER BETWEEN THE CONSCIOUS AND THE UNCONSCIOUS

The great mystics call this process calming or stilling the mind, and it means bringing every mental process under our complete control – not just on the conscious level, but in the unconscious too. For the vast majority of us, our will is operative only on the surface level. Most of us have little enough control even over our conscious mind, but the fears and hostilities and cravings that we are aware of are just the tip of the iceberg. In dreams and nightmares, we get some inkling of the strange world below the level of waking consciousness. Our fears and cravings are much stronger at this level, and we have virtually no control over them. The deepest levels of the unconscious are completely beyond our awareness, yet it is here that our problems have their taproot. In the deeper unconscious, instead of the many small fears that we are aware of on the surface level – the fear of going bald, for example, or the fear of overdrawing our checking account – there is fear itself. And here too, bound up in our unconscious conflicts, fears, and cravings, is an immense reserve of creativity, wisdom, and love.

Of course, we cannot get at the unconscious directly. We have to strengthen our will gradually and learn to extend our conscious control over deeper and deeper levels of the mind. As our will grows, we transform and harness the negative forces in consciousness, which unlocks all our vast potential. Finally, when we have eliminated all barriers between the conscious and the unconscious, we are able to move about on any level of consciousness fully aware, with our will completely operative. Mahatma Gandhi assures us that we can come to have such effortless mastery over our mind that even in our dreams a selfish thought will not arise. This is what stilling the mind means: laying to rest permanently every negative and selfish force in consciousness.

A STILL MIND

There is a popular misconception that to still the mind is to become a zombie or robot. It is just the opposite. The calmer and stiller the mind becomes, the more we can realize in our daily lives our true birthright of security, joy, and tireless energy to work for the welfare of those around us. Meher Baba, a well-known saint of modern India, used to say that a mind that is fast is sick, a mind that is slow is sound, and a mind that is still is divine. This is what the Bible means when it says, "Be still and know that I am God."

In comparing the mind to the sea, I again recall those walks my wife and I used to take every day around Lake Merritt in Oakland. Usually the wind ruffled the water, and all we could see was the surface. But on rare mornings when there was no wind and the lake was absolutely calm, we could see right down to the bottom. Similarly, when the mind is stilled, we become aware of the divine presence, the Lord of Love, who is enshrined in the very depths of our consciousness. This does not mean seeing visions or hearing voices; it means that we have had direct, immediate experience that all life is one. When we have had this experience, we will be incapable of doing anything that violates this unity of life, and we will live for the welfare of all.

THE MANTRAM IS A TRANSFORMER

If we can take advantage of all the opportunities for repeating the mantram – while waiting, while walking, while falling asleep at night – the mantram can help keep the mind calm and secure. When we are afraid or angry or driven by a strong urge for our own personal satisfaction at the expense of those around us, the mantram can transform these strong emotions into a source of tremendous positive power and help us refrain from acting or speaking impulsively. This is not repressing these powerful emotions; it is using them rather than letting them use us. The mantram has the power to turn fear into fearlessness, anger into compassion, and hatred into love.

THE ELEPHANT AND THE BAMBOO

The mantram can be of great value in learning to keep the mind even and steady, for it gives the mind something to hold on to, something to steady itself by.

In the Hindu tradition, we often compare the mind to the trunk of an elephant – restless, inquisitive, and always straying. If you watch an elephant sometime, you will see how apt the comparison is. In our towns and villages, caparisoned elephants are often taken in religious processions through the streets to the temple. The streets are crooked and narrow, lined on either side with fruit and vegetable stalls. Along comes the elephant with his restless trunk, and in one sinuous motion it grabs a whole bunch of bananas. You can almost see him asking, "What else do you expect me to do? Here is my trunk and there are the bananas." He just doesn't know what else to do with his trunk. He doesn't pause to peel the bananas, either, or to observe all the other niceties that Emily Post says should be observed in eating a banana. He takes the whole bunch, opens his cavernous mouth, and tosses the bananas in stalk and all. Then from the next stall he picks up a coconut and tosses it in after the bananas. There is a loud crack and the elephant moves on to the next stall. No threats or promises can make this restless trunk settle down.

But the wise mahout, if he knows his elephant well, will just give that trunk a short bamboo stick to hold on to before the procession starts. Then the elephant will walk along proudly with his head up high, holding the bamboo stick in front of him like a drum major with a baton. He is not interested in bananas or coconuts any more; his trunk has something to hold on to.

The mind is very much like this. Most of the time it has nothing to hold on to, but we can keep it from straying into all kinds of absurd situations if we just give it the mantram.

In my childhood, boys learning to ride an elephant always tried to get the seat near the rope around the elephant's neck. The elephant's back is broad and none too steady as he walks, so the rope is very reassuring. When the elephant spies a ripe jackfruit high in a tree and reaches up to pluck it, so that you feel like you're sitting on one of those slides on a playground, you have the rope to hang on to. When the elephant bends down for a drink of water and you find yourself almost doing a headstand, you have the rope to hang on to. In life, when you find your mind going up towards elation and what it likes or down towards depression and what it dislikes, when your habits are thwarted and your opinions are contradicted, the mantram is the rope. But it is not enough just to remember the mantram at such times, although this helps greatly. You must also be able to strengthen your will and train it to help you make the wise choices which in the long run will free the mind from these vacillations.

CHAPTER SIX

Overcoming Likes & Dislikes

A TREMENDOUS AMOUNT OF our vital energy is squandered in the vacillations of the mind as it swings towards what it likes and away from what it doesn't like. Most of us are so conditioned to go after what we like and avoid what we dislike that we do not even realize how enormous this problem is. When we are caught up in likes and dislikes, in strong opinions and rigid habits, we cannot work at our best, and we cannot know real security either. We live at the mercy of external circumstances: if things go our way, we get elated; if things do not go our way, we get depressed. It is only the mature person – the man or woman who is not conditioned by compulsive likes and dislikes, habits and opinions – who is really free in life. Such people are truly spontaneous. They can see issues clearly rather than through the distorting medium of strong opinions, and they can respond to people as they are and not as they imagine them to be.

Nothing in life is more satisfying, more masterful, than to be able to change our likes and dislikes when we need to. In fact, anyone who has mastered this skill has mastered life, and anyone who has not learned to overcome likes and dislikes is a victim of life. The statement we hear so often these days – "I like it, so I'm going to do it" – is a confession that that person is not free. When I say, "I am going to do this because I like it; I am not going to do that because I don't like it," what I am really saying is, "My hands are bound; I have no choice in life."

This is our conditioning; we have always been encouraged to do the things we like doing, to do the things we are good at doing, and not to do the things we dislike. Our nervous system has become conditioned to one-way traffic, automatically flowing towards what we like and away from what we dislike. This is very much like trying to drive a car in which the steering wheel will turn only in one direction – say, only to the left. Even the simplest maneuver, like driving to the store, would be difficult. A car like this is not only a hindrance; it is very likely to end up in a crash. When you learn to go beyond your likes and dislikes, you are freeing the wheel to turn in both directions. This is a skill which everyone can learn through repetition of the mantram and exercising the will.

MISPLACED ZEAL

The person with strong likes and dislikes will try to move away from what he does not like doing and throw himself with extravagant zeal into what he does like doing. We have a pungent story from my old state of Kerala illustrating this. Here is a farmer at harvesttime, looking at the fields of rice that must be cut, bundled, brought home, threshed, and stored. His livelihood depends on this. But it is a huge undertaking, and his will turns to jelly at the very thought of it. Then his eye falls on his bullock cart, and he notices how dilapidated it has come to look. In a flash of inspiration, he decides to paint it. The project fires him with enthusiasm. He doesn't just go to a paint store and buy a can of off-white enamel; he plans the design painstakingly, finds his own natural pigments, and mixes just the right colors with elaborate care. And then, while the rice stands in the fields still waiting to be harvested, he settles down to paint intricate floral designs on the wheels.

We are all adept at painting bullock cart wheels. When our term paper is three weeks late, we decide it is time to take apart our motorcycle. When it is time to sit down and write thank-you notes, we have an irresistible urge to reorganize our closet. When it is time to get back to work on our income tax report, we pick up a six-month-old magazine and read an article on dinosaurs with avid interest. I am not too much impressed by a person who works hard at a job he likes; what really wins my admiration is when a person is able to do a job he dislikes with cheerfulness and zest if it benefits those around him.

OVERCOMING RIGIDITY

People who have strong likes and dislikes find life very difficult; they are as rigid as if they had only one bone. Such people cannot bend, and if they are compelled to bend, they can only break. There is only one position they can take – absolute rigidity.

Today this rigidity begins to set in very early in life. In my university days, when my students would call some white-haired member of the faculty an old fogy, I used to tell them that fogyishness is not confined to any particular age group. There *are* old people who are fogies, but I have seen young fogies, too. The fogy is anyone who cannot change his opinions, who is locked into old habits and cannot yield gracefully.

Rigidity creeps up on us, and it can come very early in life. I had a friend like that even as a university student; when we would go to a restaurant, he would sit down and immediately begin to rearrange the plate, the silverware, the napkin, the glass, the chair, everything. He had a particular kind of eating arrangement which he had to work out everywhere he went. For such people there is a very apt phrase in my mother tongue. When a student isn't doing his arithmetic very well, for example, and the teacher asks why, the student replies, "I don't know; I can do it just fine under my mango tree." In other words, he is saying, "I require a particular set of conditions, and if you take me away from my mango tree, I can't even count to ten." Such a person depends for his security on external circumstances. When we go through life having to have everything just right before we can function, we will find it difficult to adjust, to be resilient, to accept any change at all.

But we can all learn to develop resilience. We can make ourselves like that Japanese doll called the daruma doll, which has a rounded base and is weighted in such a way that when you push it over, it springs back up. You can hold it down as long as you like, but as soon as you take your hand away, it jumps back up again. This is the kind of resilience that we can all cultivate. Whenever life tries to knock down people who have developed this precious quality of resilience, they are able to spring back; they have lost every trace of rigidity.

There is a strong story from the Indian tradition which shows what happens to people who cannot bend. As the Ganges river flows down from the Himalayas, it uproots big trees and carries them down into the plains. A sage noticed this and asked the river, "How is it that you tear out these huge pine trees and yet leave the willow and the reed and the tall grasses that grow by your banks?" The Ganges replied, "The pine tree doesn't know how to bend. It stands rigid and won't move out of my way, so I pull it out by the root and take it with me down to the sea. But these willows and reeds and grasses bend when I come; they do not resist me. I sing through them, and I leave them intact."

A STORY ABOUT SALT

Once rigidity has set in, we are unable to change our likes and dislikes or our opinions, no matter how disastrous it may be to go on clinging to them. For example, even though salt is known to aggravate high blood pressure, many people suffering from this condition would rather take a potent drug than reduce the amount of salt in their diet, just because they have come to like highly seasoned food. In fact, I have heard that doctors often do not even recommend to such patients that they reduce their salt intake, because they will not only fail to heed this advice but are likely to start ignoring some of the doctor's other directions as well. But I am not criticizing such people; it is extremely difficult to change our likes and dislikes without some mastery over the thinking process. It is this kind of mastery which we cultivate by repeating the mantram and learning to exercise our will.

But let me tell you a story – also about salt – which shows what artistry there is in dropping old likes and dislikes without a backward glance, and what a strong influence our personal example can be.

When I was a boy, my village doctor once put me on a salt-free diet for a year. In a tropical climate like India's, salt is very important, and it is almost impossible for most Indians to imagine food without salt or spices. So I bewailed my fate loudly. I didn't get much help from my friends at school: "No salt for a year? You might as well quit eating." My mother didn't know what to tell me either; all she could say was that it was only for one year, which didn't exactly console me. I just didn't know how I was going to get through three hundred and sixty-five days with no salt. But the next morning, as I sat down dejectedly to my first saltless breakfast, my grandmother seated herself by my side and said quietly, "I have gone off salt for a year too." And she didn't merely tolerate that saltless food; she ate it with real gusto, because she knew that her example was supporting me. As for me, I don't think I ever tasted a better meal than that saltless breakfast my grandmother shared with me. In one simple gesture, she showed her love with innate artistry. We can all learn to change our likes and dislikes like this when necessary, particularly when it is in the best interests of others, and with this capacity there comes a great sense of freedom.

CULTIVATED TASTES

It is sometimes helpful to remember that our likes and dislikes, our tastes and our opinions, however rigid they may seem now, were not always this way. Very often we have worked hard to acquire a particular like, to cultivate a particular taste. Let me take just one example which must be familiar to all of you: beer. In my university days in India, as a professor of English literature, I used to read in many plays and novels about the glories of beer – what a marvelous beverage it is, what conviviality it evokes. And so one day a friend and I decided that we would have to try this beer for ourselves. We went to a place frequented by the British, sat down nonchalantly like men of the world, and placed our order. The waiter brought us a big bottle, opened it for us with a flourish, and stood back to enjoy the show. We never knew there was any special art to pouring beer, so when we poured it, it foamed and foamed. In a few seconds the glass was full of foam and there was only a little liquid at the bottom. When we finally managed to get the beer to our lips through all that foam, we just couldn't believe how bitter it was. We couldn't take more than a few swallows of the stuff. This was the drink whose praises I heard sung so lavishly! Now I have tremendous respect for anyone who can control his palate enough to learn not only to drink beer but to enjoy it, too. Anyone who has put that much effort into acquiring a taste should certainly be able to put that same effort into setting himself free from the tyranny of likes and dislikes too.

TACKLING JOBS WE DISLIKE

The way to tackle a job you dislike is by giving it more of your attention. This may sound simple, but let me assure you that it is very effective. We are under the impression that it is the job itself which is either interesting or boring. Now, to a certain extent this is true. But it is even truer that it is the quality or the intensity of the attention we give a job that makes it interesting or not. In other words, if we can concentrate fully, we can make almost any job interesting. Full concentration brings relaxation and joy. It is the struggle of divided attention that brings a great deal of the misery that we associate with jobs we don't like.

When we get a job we don't like, most of us protest that we are artists, that this job is drudgery and we require work which challenges our creative talents. Very often this is just a euphemistic way of saying that the job is one we don't like doing. If the job is one that really needs to be done, stifle your protests, repeat the mantram, and get to work. If we can just give more of our attention to work we dislike, we find that it becomes tolerable and even interesting. Giving our full attention works wonders with any task. Suppose you have to clear away some weeds in the backyard. Don't think about how hot it is, how tired you are, or how much you'd rather be at the pool; remind yourself that the weeds are unsightly, they are a fire hazard, and *someone* has to do the job. You don't just take a few listless whacks at the first weed and then wander off, either; instead, you get to work. You feel a real sense of accomplishment as the weeds fall, and soon you are seeking them out: "Aha, there's another one behind the steps!" Finally you get so absorbed that if someone brings out a glass of lemonade for you, you find yourself saying, "Thanks, but I can't stop now." By giving it your full attention, you have turned a job you detested into work that you find rewarding, and you have strengthened your will in the bargain.

Another way to free ourselves from likes and dislikes is not to put off the jobs we dislike. Most of us have been conditioned to do the jobs we like first; we leave the disagreeable job for last. My grandmother sometimes used to ask me to do something important, but I had so many unimportant things of my own to attend to that the task she had entrusted to me didn't always get done. When she would ask, "When are you going to do it?" I would answer, "One of these days, Granny." She wasn't impressed. "One of these days is none of these days." When you hear someone say, "I'm going to get around to it one of these days," you can be sure that it isn't going to get done. The mark of the mature person is the capacity to take up a job immediately – "forthwith," as Jesus says – and do it cheerfully and with concentration.

When we postpone a disagreeable job, we may be wishing that it will miraculously vanish if we ignore it long enough. But jobs we put off have a way of not vanishing – in fact, they have a way of getting more difficult with the passage of time. In this connection, my grandmother used to say, "He who post-pones will have to carry a mountain on his back." Months ago that loose hinge on the screen door would have taken only a few minutes to fix; now the other hinge has worked loose and the door has fallen off in the wind, and torn the screen as well. We could have started our term paper weeks ago and worked on it steadily all along, but now there's just three days left, not only to write our term paper but to study for the final and read all the books for the course too. When we postpone things in this way, things pile up and we end up carrying a mountain of work which we could have avoided very easily.

HOW TO BEGIN

How do we begin a job that we have been putting off, espe-cially one that we have been dreading? People have often asked me for some simple secret. "It is so overwhelming," they say. "Where do we begin?" A frontal assault is very difficult; even with the best of intentions, we often can't just sit down and start composing the opening paragraph of our long-over-due term paper. But there is a simple trick that works. Repeat the mantram a few times and take a deep breath; then clear off your desk, sharpen your pencil, pull out the books you need, and spread out your notes *as if* you were going to get to work. When your mind complains, "I just can't face it," reas-sure it that you are just going to leaf through the books, sort the notes, and push the pencil around a little. Then, to play fair and keep your mind at ease, you do just that: leaf through the books a little, sort your notes, jot down a stray idea that occurs to you – it doesn't really much matter what. Soon, despite your lack of intentions, there is another stray idea; then, as you skim a page, a couple of ideas fall into place, and you read a little further and get a few more ideas and write down some new insights. Before you know it, you have become absorbed in the project: there is enthusiasm, there is a steady flow of ideas, and you are working with real concentration. You must have noticed how step by step you can get embroiled in little jobs you hadn't set out to do; here, you are putting that same tendency to work for you instead of letting it work against you. This is the way to get the job done; it helps concentration and it strengthens the will.

LEARNING TO DROP A JOB AT WILL

This ability to drop something we like at will is a very important step in freeing ourselves from likes and dislikes. When we are doing a job we dislike, we can drop it on the slightest pretext without a second thought. But just see how difficult this is when we are compulsively caught up in something! When we are reading our favorite author or working on our pet project and something comes up which demands more urgent attention, it is very difficult for the mind to drop what it is absorbed in. And in the evening, when we leave our office or our campus, our work comes running after us, yapping like a little terrier at our heels. We don't really taste our dinner, we don't really hear what our family and friends are saying to us, we don't really perceive the needs of others, all because this little terrier keeps yapping in the back of our minds. It is good to work hard and apply ourselves completely to our work, but we should never let ourselves be driven by it.

All too often, once we have let ourselves get obsessed with some job – say, writing a report the boss has asked for at work – we aren't able to get the thought of it out of our minds. While we are showering we find ourselves composing clever topic sentences; while walking along the street we find ourselves thinking of an apt statistic to work in; while falling asleep we see a better way to organize everything. These are all excellent times to repeat the mantram. You will be freeing yourself from the constant burden of your project, and you will find that repeating the mantram at such times actually improves your performance when you are able to get back to work again.

Learning to drop work at a moment's notice is one of the great spiritual disciplines practiced in Catholic convents and monasteries. Saint Thérèse of Lisieux tells us that when the bell for prayer rang, she trained herself to put down her sewing without even finishing the stitch she was on. Imagine the patience and effort required to master this art of dropping work without so much as a ripple of protest in the mind! Most of us, when we are caught in something we like and we hear the call for dinner, say, "Oh, all right; just let me finish the page I'm reading." And we probably read a few pages more in the bargain.

When we haven't learned to drop our work at will like this, our concentration suffers, our work suffers, and even our personal relationships suffer. When we have turned over in our mind the possible solutions to a problem for the fiftieth time, the fifty-first time is not likely to be any more productive. In fact, it only consumes more of our vital energy as the mind runs on and on out of control. This is the time to remember the mantram. If we can just quit worrying about all the possible solutions, which the mantram can help us to do, we will often find that a better solution than any we had yet thought of will pop up from a deeper level of consciousness – perhaps even as we are saying the mantram.

In this connection, let me share with you a simple secret about memory. If you find yourself unable to recall some fact, some name, some line of poetry, don't stop and grit your teeth trying to remember it; this will only disrupt your train of thought. Just drop your attachment to remembering it, repeat the mantram a couple of times, and proceed without it, unconcerned. Soon the fact, the name, the line of poetry will be tugging at your sleeve saying, "Here I am – 'William the Conqueror, 1066.'"

When you find your mind persistently dogged by thoughts of your work, your project, your plans – especially at night, when you can't sleep – repeating the mantram can help you drop these nagging thoughts completely. This is a skill that will help your concentration, improve your peace of mind, help you to free yourself from compulsive likes and dislikes, and contribute greatly to strengthening your will – and it is a skill which everyone can develop through the help of the mantram and persistent practice.

FREEDOM IN PERSONAL RELATIONSHIPS

People with strong likes and dislikes are often extremely self-centered; and they often have difficulties in personal relationships. There is trouble because sooner or later the person with strong likes and dislikes will gravitate towards another person with equally strong likes and dislikes who will contradict him. When people with fierce likes and dislikes are contradicted – which is absolutely inevitable – a host of disastrous consequences ensue. Personal relationships deteriorate, emotional security vanishes, there is constant mental turmoil, and all sorts of psychosomatic problems arise: breathing problems, digestive problems, allergies, and even cardiovascular problems. So you can see that freeing ourselves from the tyranny of likes and dislikes is not just of theoretical importance. It can solve emotional problems and often physical problems as well, and it never fails to make for richer personal relationships.

This last point is of utmost importance in our modern age, which often seems to me to be the age of loneliness. Being able to go beyond your own likes and dislikes helps immensely in restoring the personal relationships that make life worth living, for it enables us to be patient, cheerful, and loving with those around us.

Freeing ourselves from compulsive likes and dislikes is essential for cooperation anywhere, whether in the home or in the office, and cooperation is the perfect antidote to deteriorating relationships. Competition, on the other hand, can only divide us.

Competition is in the very air today, on the international

scene as well as in the office, on the campus, and in the home. Comparing ourselves with others, envying others, only aggravates competition. What we forget when we envy others is that every job, every position, every role has some element of drudgery, some unpleasant aspect or heavy responsibility. The way we should evaluate a job is not to ask what we like about it or dislike about it, whether it pays better than our partner's or is more prestigious; what we should ask is, does it contribute to the welfare of others? If it does, it is a good job, and there is no need to compare it to what others do.

When we are tempted to compete and compare ourselves with others, the mantram can come to our rescue. If we can repeat the mantram when we find ourselves falling into competitiveness and invidious comparison, it will help greatly to keep our minds calm and our relationships secure.

CHAPTER SEVEN

Excitement & Depression

EXCITEMENT AND DEPRESSION are words we hear constantly these days. It almost seems as if everyone you meet is either going into a depression or just coming out – if he or she is not in a depression right now. We have come to look upon this cycle as a necessary part of life.

At the same time, we cultivate excitement everywhere – exciting vacations to the Bahamas, exciting new career possibilities, even exciting breakfast cereals. We are constantly being conditioned to seek excitement as the quintessence of life. Television, movies, and popular music all go on repeating the message that unless life is exciting, it is dull and drab.

The problem is that excitement never lasts. It is the nature of the mind to change. If we think life is drab when we're not elated, if we feel alive only when exhilarated, then we are bound to feel depressed when excitement fades. It is one of the laws of nature that what goes up must come down; so we should not be surprised that in a culture that prizes excitement, depression in some form or other is practically epidemic.

In both phases of this cycle, whether we are feeling elated or

dejected, the mind is racing out of our control. The only difference is whether it is racing over what is pleasant or what
is unpleasant. The dejected person may look passive, but his
mind may be just as active and agitated as that of the excited
person who is running around gesticulating and speaking
wildly. One sign of this is the inability to concentrate. When
the mind is agitated, attention is scattered and concentration
almost impossible. That is why the person who is prone to
the cycle of excitement and depression often finds it hard to
be effective at work, steadfast in personal relationships, and
secure within.

Most people have little objection to getting excited. It is
excitement's morbid sibling that we never want to see. But if
we court elation, we are courting depression also. The more we
seek excitement, the more likely it is that depression will follow. To avoid feeling depressed, we need to keep off the whole
sad-go-round of elation and depression altogether. We need
to learn to keep our mind on an even keel.

Our culture places such a premium on excitement that this
advice is most unwelcome. "Don't let yourself get excited" has
an unpleasant, puritanical ring. But that is simply because we
believe the only alternative to excitement is a flat, monotonous
life. In fact, there is a third state which is neither excitement
nor depression, but far, far above both: a quiet sense of abiding joy which is our real nature. Only when we taste this joy, I
would say, can we really enjoy life. If we could only slow down
enough to observe ourselves objectively when we are excited,

we would see that we are not in a position to enjoy anything at such times; the mind is much too frantic.

When you are able to see the specter of depression lurking behind excitement and get some taste of the joy which transcends both, you will come to look upon excitement with profound suspicion. I remember once seeing the picture of the winner of a lottery, taken at the instant he heard that he had won. The man's face was contorted in excitement. It was a most unpleasant, agonized look, of pain rather than joy, just the opposite of enjoyment. Whenever the mind races like this, it hides the natural beauty of the human face beneath an ugly mask. We see the mature reaction to success in a wise statement attributed to the late President Kennedy. On the day of his inauguration, a reporter asked him, "Mr. President, aren't you very excited on this great occasion?" Kennedy replied, "No, not excited – very interested."

DIFFERENT FACES OF EXCITEMENT

People abandon themselves to excitement in different ways. Some begin to talk and talk. Their ship has come home, their horse has won, their article has been accepted for publication, and they have to let everybody know. They pick up the telephone and call people they haven't seen in six months to tell them the good news, not because they are interested in what the other person has to say but because they must find an opportunity to express their excitement. Other people begin to find everything inordinately funny, and will laugh at the slightest provocation. Wholesome laughter is a welcome relaxation, when it is not at anyone else's expense, but the wild laughter of excitement only leaves us prone to irritability later on.

Some people make elaborate plans or have grandiose visions of the future. If they have written a poem and someone praises it, it is only a matter of time before they envision their book of verse going into its tenth printing and crowds of admirers fighting to get their autograph; next they are composing their acceptance speech for the Nobel Prize. Perhaps saddest of all, there are people who respond to excitement with a flood of self-confidence, with plans and dreams far beyond their capacity to realize. They drive themselves to work harder and harder; they can't bear to hear their opinions contradicted or their plans and ambitions questioned; yet a short time later, when depression has struck, they will be doubting everything they do.

THE PENDULUM

Whatever form excitement takes, it is only agitation, a storm in the mind which we have been conditioned to regard as pleasant. When the mind oscillates wildly over good news, over pleasant prospects and unlimited possibilities, all this means is that we are dwelling more on ourselves and forgetting the needs of those around us. And once we have set the pendulum of the mind swinging, the inevitable reaction has to set in sooner or later. When that happens, we will still be dwelling on ourselves, but only on what is negative: the bad news, the unpleasant prospects, how ineffectual we are.

I used to see this as a professor in India, when I was in charge of the debating society. When we won a debate, some of the students would get so excited that their bodies would be trembling and they wouldn't be able to speak coherently. The next day they would be sleeping in class, and when I would rouse them to ask why they weren't able to keep awake, they would reply, "I couldn't get to sleep last night." Some of the brighter students would make the connection and add, "Maybe our winning the debate wasn't so good after all." "No," I used to answer, "winning the debate was fine. It was your reaction to it which made it impossible for you to sleep."

GUARDING AGAINST DEPRESSION

All of us can guard ourselves against these wild swings of the mind by taking a few simple steps. "Simple" here does not mean easy. As I keep repeating, everything around us is telling us to do just the opposite of what I have found helpful in my own experience. Fortunately, keeping the mind steady is a skill that anyone can learn, and even a little effort helps greatly in damping the wild pendulum swings of the mind.

The most effective of these steps, of course, is not to get elated when things are going our way, and the best way to accomplish this is to repeat the mantram at such times and keep trying to free ourselves from rigid likes and dislikes. Whenever we reduce the tyranny of likes and dislikes, of habits and opinions, we are helping to safeguard ourselves against depression. Then, whether we win the Irish sweepstakes or our horse finishes last, the pendulum of the mind will not be set in motion. Whether things go our way or someone else's, we can always repeat the mantram and remain calm.

It is important to do this whenever things are going against us, but it is even more important when things are going for us, when excitement is rising and everything looks wonderful. In other words, do not wait for depression to come knocking at the door. It is difficult to remember to stay calm and repeat the mantram in the face of excitement, I admit, but it is far more difficult once depression has set in. This may sound like the advice of a killjoy, but in the end it will save you much suffering. Not only that, repeating the mantram at such times actually allows you to enjoy these moments in freedom, for when the mind is extremely excited, it is too busy swinging to and fro to be able to find joy.

When fortune smiles on you, when everyone agrees with you, when you get an unexpected opportunity to do something you like, these are all times you can repeat the mantram. When you hear good news, the mantram will consolidate your joy. When someone praises you, repeating the mantram will keep the praise from going to your head. Then, when someone criticizes you – as they must, sooner or later, because that is the nature of life – you will be able to consider the criticism objectively and not get depressed over it. If the praise is warranted, you can be appreciative; if the criticism is valid, you should act on it; but under no circumstances should you let praise or blame throw you into agitation. This is where the mantram comes to your rescue.

LIVING IN THE PRESENT

Looking forward too much to some kind of excitement in the future is another way of courting depression. Some of my friends tell me that as children they used to look forward so much to opening their presents on Christmas morning that they could hardly sleep the night before. Then, as soon as they opened the last package, depression began to set in. A few well-chosen presents for our children at Christmas are an appropriate way of showing love, but if we really love our children, we will do our very best not to let them get excited about the future and what it will bring them. Not only will this guard them against the depression that is sure to follow; it will help them develop a capacity for joy that is not subject to disappointment.

When we mortgage the present for the future, we are not only asking for depression in the future; we are also deadening ourselves to the present. Just see how many of us, if there is a big party to go to in the evening, go through our work that day with one eye on the clock, thinking, "Only six hours more; only five and a half hours more." We can wish away the whole week looking forward to a weekend of skiing; we can wish away the whole year looking forward to a vacation. And when we go on saying, "I can't wait to be twenty-one," or to get married, or to get promoted, or to retire, we can wish away an entire life.

With vacations, for example, we work for fifty weeks at our jobs looking forward to two exciting weeks in Acapulco or the Bahamas. All our expectation is on those two weeks, so our job seems like drudgery; our home life is humdrum. Expectation mounts as the vacation draws near: we plan, we pack, we talk. Then for two frantic weeks we are determined to have a good time, even if it kills us. When we get back, there should be an ambulance waiting to take us to the intensive care unit. All we have to show for this is a few slides, a bad sunburn, and a towel from the Hotel Ritz. We go back to our same old routine, which seems duller than ever, and soon we are looking forward to next year's vacation. I respond much more to Mahatma Gandhi's idea of a vacation. He was asked by a Western journalist, "Mr. Gandhi, you have been working fifteen hours a day, seven days a week, for fifty years. Why don't you take a vacation?" Gandhi's reply was, "I am always on vacation." We can make every day a vacation by getting away from preoccupation with ourselves and our own personal satisfactions. We learn to do this by thinking more of the needs of others and by repeating the mantram in order to keep our mind even, to shed our likes and dislikes, and to drop our problems at will.

GETTING OUT OF A DEPRESSION

In all of this, of course, I am talking about the everyday, garden-variety lows to which all of us are subject. Clinical depression, by contrast, can be quite dangerous, and medical intervention may call for drug therapy in the hands of an experienced physician to stabilize mood swings and make the condition manageable. Many physicians, however, are concerned that such drugs are being overused, prescribed in response to pressure from patients, who may even consider this kind of therapy fashionable. More and more, they warn, we are becoming a society in which life's inevitable downturns are met by popping a pill. But ups and downs are the very texture of life, and mind-stabilizing drugs, over time, may actually weaken the inner resources we need to master whatever life sends us. When we go on unnecessarily suppressing ordinary mood swings with a powerful drug, we may be suppressing our capacity for creativity, for sensitivity to others, for drawing on our own deeper resources to go beyond the mood swings of excitement and depression and find real peace of mind.

Fortunately, when we find ourselves in a depression, all is not lost. There are a number of things we can do ourselves. It is the nature of depression for the mind to dwell on itself – on one's problems, one's failures, one's inadequacies. If we can distract the mind from this favorite pastime – trick it, if you like, into turning its attention to something nobler – we may find that we are no longer depressed.

One of the most important steps to take is not to spend any time trying to analyze your depression to see how it came about. This just feeds the depression, and even if you are able to pinpoint a cause, the depression will still be with you. In fact, when the mind is depressed, it simply is incapable of seeing clearly. Everything is a house of mirrors, and the more you think about the causes, the more depressed you are likely to be. But when you are actually in a depression, it doesn't really matter what the cause is, any more than it matters at the time what made your car go into a skid. The important thing is that the mind, like the car, is out of control, and that you need to act immediately in order to get control of it again.

Here, of course, the direct approach simply will not work. You cannot say, "I know I just feel depressed because I didn't get that raise, so I hereby shake this depression off." The mind will only laugh at you. Instead, whenever you are tempted to think about how depressed you are and why, go out for a fast walk repeating the mantram in your mind. When you can give your full attention to the mantram, there will be no attention left for your problems, which means that the depression has packed its bags and left town. At the beginning you will find this very difficult to do. The mind will slip away from the mantram again and again. But keep on trying; after a while the mantram will take hold, which means that the car of your mind is back on the road again and ready to come under control.

In fighting depression the mantram needs all the help it can get, and the most effective support we can offer is to throw ourselves into work or activities that turn our attention outward and keep us from thinking about ourselves. The harder and more challenging the job is, the better, especially if it benefits those around us. Hard physical work is excellent, and it is particularly effective in the company of other people. As you cultivate the precious capacity to turn your attention outward like this and to give your full attention to something that benefits others, depression will find you a less and less attractive host. Eventually it will give you up altogether and say, "Let me go find someone who is prepared to pay me the attention I am used to having."

Unfortunately, when people are depressed they usually do just the opposite of this. They hide themselves in their room, draw the curtains, and minimize the distractions so the mind can dwell on its problems without interruption. Often they feel they don't want to inflict their depression on others. This may be a commendable motive for withdrawing, but it only makes the depression worse.

In India I once had a friend who used to withdraw this way when depression struck him. He was a very cultured, prosperous man and quite an entertaining person to be with, a good conversationalist and very hospitable – until he fell into a depression. For months he would go on being his usual entertaining self; then, abruptly, he would fall into a depression. He wouldn't talk to anyone in a civil manner; he wouldn't come out of his house; he wouldn't invite anyone in. This, too, used to go on for months. At last, when he was in the midst of one of these terrible depressions, I went to his house to see him. He had instructed his butler to tell callers that he was not at home, but I knew that he was; so before the butler could shut the door, I had slipped inside and started for my friend's room. I couldn't believe that it was the same man. His features were frozen in self-hatred, and he had nothing but hostility towards the whole world. He was furious when he saw me, and began using some strong language to drive me out. When he saw that words couldn't drive me out, he actually pushed me out the door. Now, I knew that this was not really my friend; it was just some virus that had taken control of him – and I knew how to deal with it, too. So I pushed my way back in, and I was able to stay and talk to him and finally help him. Afterwards he used to boast to people, "I even pushed him out of my house, but he cared so much for me that he came right back in."

Another bit of advice for coping with depression is simple, difficult, and extremely powerful: always act as if you were not depressed. People in a depression walk slowly, with their heads down; they slump in their chairs with a preoccupied look in their eyes. They avoid being with people, and when they have to be with people they avoid talking to them or meeting their eyes. They may be so absorbed in themselves that they do not even see or hear what is going on around them. So when you are in a depression, make every effort to be with people and let them draw you out. Walk briskly with your head up. Try to take an interest in what is going on around you, and smile at people and talk to them even if you don't feel like it. Before you know it, you will find that you are not pretending to be cheerful any longer; you really are cheerful, because you have forgotten yourself. Of course, it takes a good deal of willpower to turn outward like this when everything inside you is crying to withdraw. But here again, the mantram can come to your rescue. It will strengthen your will and enable you to remember that depression is just a habit which can be unlearned just as it was learned.

SPONTANEITY

Sometimes when I offer this advice people tell me, "That sounds artificial. Isn't it being dishonest to act differently from how you feel? I don't want to be artificial; I want to be natural and spontaneous. I don't want to be hypocritical; I want to be true to myself." We are not being hypocritical when we act cheerful. Depression is not our real condition; it is only a mask. Our real nature is abiding joy.

Everyone wants to be spontaneous these days, but very few seem to realize what spontaneity really is. Most of us act as if spontaneity means "doing your own thing": doing just what we like, when we like, and in the way we like. If the sky is blue and the sun is warm, we skip our classes or call our place of work to say that we won't be coming in. If we don't like a friend's new car, we say so; after all, it's a free country, isn't it? We indulge excitement on any pretext, and feel "down" without any apparent reason. What we are pleased to call spontaneity here, if I may be blunt, is simply doing what we feel like doing and not doing what we don't feel like doing. When we live this way, we are really no more spontaneous than a rubber ball which bounces when we drop it on the sidewalk; we are simply reacting as we have been conditioned to react. Real spontaneity lies in being able to overcome years of powerful conditioning in order to express the abiding joy and infinite love which is our real nature. We are being truly spontaneous when we can change the habits of a lifetime overnight and not be oppressed by it. We are being truly spontaneous when we are able to drop our pet project and work for the welfare of those around us without a ripple of protest in the mind. We are being truly spontaneous when we can respond calmly, constructively, and compassionately to others when they are hostile to us.

It is not possible to attain spontaneity by doing only what we like, or postponing disagreeable jobs, or moving away from people who irritate us. When we do this, we are just drifting through life, following the course of least resistance. The Compassionate Buddha describes the spiritual life as "going against the current" – learning to go against our past conditioning. By just drifting, we will never cross the sea of life to the far shore of abiding joy.

This "drifting" approach to spontaneous living reminds me of the little vegetable garden I planted when I first came to Berkeley. I didn't know anything about gardening, but one of my friends, a congenial Englishman, offered me advice and support. He was of the spontaneous school of gardening: the garden can take care of itself; you just put the seeds in the ground and come back in a few months to gather in the harvest. When I suggested that perhaps I should weed a little too, he used to tell me, "The weeds deserve their chance too, old boy." This was certainly an easy way to garden – effortless, in fact – but when autumn came, all that I harvested was one small ear of corn and a couple of shriveled tomatoes. This is exactly what happens with the garden of the mind. If we just let it grow any old way, we will get a bumper harvest of weeds, thistles, and brambles. But if we take care to cultivate wisely and weed out what is not so wise, our effort will produce a rich harvest in more abundant vitality, deeper personal relationships, and the resilience to face any challenge life may bring our way.

The secret of spontaneity is training; this is how we undo our conditioning. Look at the effortless grace with which a great artist or a great athlete performs. They make the most amazing feat look so simple that we think we all could do it, but we know that behind all their ease and grace are years of dedication, practice, and sustained effort. No one expects to be able to step onto the court at Wimbledon the first time she picks up a tennis racquet, or to play Beethoven's concerto in Carnegie Hall the first time he picks up a violin. It is just the same with the mind. We cannot just decide to be spontaneous; we cannot change our likes and dislikes or banish depression from our lives overnight; but we can all make these marvelous transformations in our consciousness if we are prepared to put in the sustained effort they require.

Any effort we make to keep the mind steady helps on all fronts. If we can drop our work at will, we will be much less liable to depression. If we can bear with those who irritate us, we will find it easier not to postpone necessary jobs. If we can juggle with our likes and dislikes, we can easily drop our work and even our problems at will. And whenever we repeat the mantram, we are helping to keep the mind calm and steady, which helps us to do everything in greater freedom. Even if we do nothing more than try to keep the mind steady during the ups and downs of the day, we are deepening our awareness of life far more than we know.

CHAPTER EIGHT

Harnessing Fear, Anger, & Greed

WHEN THE BIBLE says, "As a man thinketh in his heart, so is he," it is telling us that the key to intentional living is in gaining mastery over the mind. The Compassionate Buddha puts the same message precisely in the famous Twin Verses:

> All that we are is the result of what we have thought:
> we are formed and molded by our thoughts. Those
> whose minds are shaped by selfish thoughts cause mis-
> ery when they speak or act. Sorrows roll over them as
> the wheels of a cart roll over the tracks of the bullock
> that draws it.

> All that we are is the result of what we have thought:
> we are formed and molded by our thoughts. Those
> whose minds are shaped by selfless thoughts give joy
> whenever they speak or act. Joy follows them like a
> shadow that never leaves them.

"Thought" here is not just the thoughts we think with the conscious mind. It includes the workings of the unconscious as well, our fears and desires and worries and loves and aspirations. Most of the time, the vast majority of us live on the surface level of consciousness, not suspecting the storms that rage in our unconscious. We get some hint of the tremendous power of these storms when they break through to the surface in the form of fear, anger, and greed. When these get out of control, they can pick us up and hurl us about as they like, exactly as if some force takes us over and makes us do things, say things, that we would not ordinarily do.

Take fear, for example. Fear of snakes is part of our consciousness in rural India; when a villager is walking home in the twilight and sees a snake on the path ahead of him – it may not even be a real snake, just a bit of coiled-up rope – he gives a jump that would make any Olympic athlete envious. If he had stood calmly and said, "Let me see how far I can jump," he would not have been able to cover even half that distance. Fear gives him access to a deeper level of consciousness, where he finds the power to jump.

Fear plays a valuable role here if it enables the villager to avoid being bitten by the snake, but most of the time fear, anger, and greed serve no useful purpose. They are simply power going to waste – or worse, power being used destructively. If we take an honest look at our behavior under the influence of fear or anger or the compulsion of greed, we have to admit that it is not very pretty; it is not something we are very proud of. Here is where the mantram is an invaluable ally. It can harness all this destructive power that is going to waste and transform it: fear into fearlessness, anger into compassion, and greed into the desire to be of service to those around us. It is very much like harnessing any source of power. Wind, for example, can be a devastating natural force. A hurricane can sweep away thousands of lives and leaves utter desolation behind it. Yet the same energy, wind, can be harnessed to generate electricity to light people's homes.

WHEN ANGER, FEAR, OR GREED IS SWEEPING YOU AWAY

The simplest thing to do when you are caught by fear, anger, or greed is to go for a long, fast walk repeating the mantram. This may sound simplistic, but try it. Go for a fast walk repeating *Rama, Rama, Rama* or *Jesus, Jesus, Jesus* in your mind, and you will find that the relationship between the rhythm of your breathing, the rhythm of your footsteps, and the rhythm of the mantram has a deep influence on your consciousness. Recently a friend of mine told me she had discovered that when she was upset, if she could hold on to the mantram for twenty minutes while she walked, it could transform any negative emotion. "When I realized that," she said, "I realized that any transformation is possible." You may not always be able to afford the luxury of going for a fast walk, but you can repeat the mantram any time. With practice you will find that when some negative emotion rises like a tidal wave in your mind, you don't have to be flung up onto the beach or pounded down against the bottom of the sea as in the old days; you can ride the wave on the mantram board with your arms spread wide. Once you have learned this skill, there is a tremendous sense of mastery.

Fear and anger and greed agitate the mind; they churn the mind up like a stormy sea. When your mind is heaving up and down, it may be difficult to hold on to the mantram if your mantram is long. For emergencies like this, I would recommend using a shortened form of the mantram, the kernel of the mantram: *Rama* if your mantram is *Hare Rama Hare Rama; Om* if it is *Om mani padme hum; Jesus* if you use some form of the Jesus Prayer such as *Lord Jesus Christ* or *Lord Jesus Christ, have mercy on me.* This kernel of the mantram is the most potent word in the holy name; it is short and simple. No matter how agitated your mind is, you can hang on to it while it does its work of harnessing and transforming the power that was rampaging in you.

WORRY

When you are afraid, repeat the mantram; it has the power to change fear into fearlessness. For people who claim that fear is not a problem for them, I simply ask if they have any worries. The usual answer is, "More than I can count." Worries are simply little fears; put a hundred worries together and you have one big fear. When your vitality leaks out through a hundred little worries, it is no wonder that you feel inadequate to the challenges of the day. So repeat the mantram when you are worried, and it will change worry into confidence. The same goes for the rest of fear's poor relations: the mantram protects you not only against worry, but also against anxiety, nervousness, and apprehension.

When I was at the University of Minnesota many years ago,

where I spent the winter and lived to tell the tale, I had a young friend from my old state of Kerala whose finals were beginning. One subject was particularly difficult for him, and his scholarship depended on getting straight As. He was a good student, but as happens on the eve of finals, he became very anxious and his memory began to play tricks on him. He knocked on my door and asked if I had some immediate help for somebody who was facing a final exam. I have no objection to being made a last resort, and I didn't ask him about his spiritual beliefs or his philosophical background. I knew the tradition from which his family came, so I gave him the mantram used in that tradition and took him for a walk from Minneapolis to Saint Paul and back again, along the banks of the Mississippi River, six miles to and six miles fro. Every time he would say, "I'm tired; can't we stop?" I would tell him, "Just keep repeating your mantram." When we got back to the dormitory, he was so completely relaxed that I just opened the door and pushed him in; he went straight in and fell into his bed and slept soundly. As I said, he had been a good student, so he went to his finals the next morning rested and with a quiet assurance, and did very well.

ANXIETY

Many different things can make us anxious. Take the example of public speaking with which I began this book. Public speaking, it seems, causes anxiety universally, and this anxiety expresses itself in many unpleasant ways. When you have to speak on the platform, if you are not used to it, you see what interesting things can happen. Suddenly you will find your hands swelling. You try to put them in your pockets; they won't go in. Something happens to your larynx, you have strange flutterings in your stomach, a little mouse seems to be running up and down your spinal column, and your legs turn to rubber. These are all experiences which many aspiring speakers – including myself – have undergone, and one of the easiest remedies is to repeat the mantram.

When you go for a job interview and you get the butterfly effect, try the mantram. When you go to the dentist, or to the doctor, or to a hospital, these are all occasions to repeat the mantram. Use the mantram when you are in pain; it will take your mind off the pain, whereas fear only makes pain worse.

When you are fearful and keep dwelling on yourself, that naturally impedes the healing process, but when you switch your mind over to the mantram, your body is able to go about its work of healing unimpeded.

BIGGER FEARS

When you are faced with a really big fear, it can unify your consciousness, and at a time like that, the mantram can go in very deep. A friend of mine works as a doctor in the intensive care unit of a local hospital, and she had as a patient an elderly woman who was seriously ill, so ill that she wasn't even able to breathe except with the aid of one of those breathing machines, a respirator. The patient was a Catholic, so my friend suggested that she repeat *Hail Mary*. She began doing it and her condition improved considerably. In this case, the mantram helped more than anything else that had been tried, because it helped the patient deal with her fear.

Unfortunately, there are people who remember the mantram when they are afraid but stop using it when the danger is past. We have a story in India about how a person crossing a shaky bridge says *Rama, Rama, Rama* for all he is worth, but as soon as he is back on terra firma again it is *kama, kama, kama* – *kama* stands for selfish desires. Many people are like this. It would be better to have been using the mantram all along; then, in the face of great fear, the mantram will be right there at your side, reminding you that there is Someone inside who is your protector.

ANGER

Whenever I talk about using the mantram to transform fear and anger, people nod approvingly as long as I am talking about fear. After all, no one wants to be fearful; no one wants to worry. But the nods of approval often stop when I ask people to repeat the mantram in moments of anger. "You're not asking us to repress anger?" they ask. "Isn't it better to express anger than to repress it?" This is a legitimate question, but it is based on the assumption that we have only two choices where anger is concerned: expression or repression. Either way, anger eventually works against us, undermining our relationships, our security, and even our health. But there is a third alternative: we can transform anger, through the repetition of the mantram. Anger is power, and the mantram can transform this negative power into its positive counterpart, which is compassion. Not only that, the very power that is behind anger serves to drive the mantram even deeper into our consciousness.

THE AGE OF ANGER

Anger is so endemic today that our century could be called the age of anger. There is even a cult surrounding anger, which conditions us to regard the angry person as powerful and dynamic and free. This is how anger is shown in books, in movies, on television, everywhere, and we have come to believe it. There are workshops now where people are taught to express their anger more freely, where they are taught that when someone gets angry with them, the way to gain control of the situation is to get angry in return. In fact, in our day, anger is considered to be part of expressing oneself, a vital means of communication.

THE DAMAGE ANGER DOES

But if you have the detachment, take a good look at what anger actually does. When someone gets angry with you and you get angry in return, is this really expressing yourself, or are you just dancing to the tune they are calling? And the angry words that you hurl at your partner, or your parents, or your children – even if you think they clear the air, they will rankle for a long time in the other person's consciousness, which scarcely contributes to better personal relations.

All too often it is those we are emotionally entangled with that are the targets of our anger: they are nearby, so we lash out. If getting angry actually cemented personal relations, I would be all for it. But this anger only drives a wedge into the relationship, and each time we get angry we are making the split deeper and deeper. The words we say in anger, the decisions we make in anger, the things we do in anger – none of these are likely to be wise. There is a chilling statistic that over seventy percent of murder victims are friends or relatives of the murderer, slain in anger often over what started out as trifling quarrels – and often, ironically, with firearms that were in the house to protect the occupants from intruders from outside.

Finally, see what damage the angry person is doing to himself. My grandmother used to say that getting angry was like swallowing a lighted firecracker. The angry person may hurl barbed words and even throw things, but it is he who really gets hurt – by developing serious physical problems like asthma, high blood pressure, and heart disease. When you keep letting yourself get angry, you wear an anger rut in your consciousness; the anger response becomes habitual. You have become anger-prone, and anger-prone people, wherever they go in life, will always find some obliging person to step on their corns or contradict their pet opinion. For such people, steadfast relationships and emotional security become impossible.

HARNESSING ANGER'S POWER

There is a tremendous statement in the Hindu scriptures: "That which makes you sick, if harnessed, can be that which makes you well." When I say that anger makes us sick, it is not an exaggeration, and I am pleased to see that the medical profession is slowly coming around to this view of anger. In a medical journal not long ago I read an article by an American doctor titled something like "The Therapeutic Value of Charity" – charity in the New Testament sense of love, forbearance, forgiveness. This doctor cites a number of case histories of men and women who developed some very serious physical problems after prolonged bouts of anger and resentment, including strokes and heart attacks precipitated by violent outbursts of temper. This is anger making us sick. But when we can harness the power in anger, the same power that was making us ill can give us the capacity to work tirelessly to relieve the distress of those around us. Health and security come our way on both the physical and the emotional level when we forget ourselves in working for some selfless goal.

An angry person is allowing power to rise against him and enslave him, but when he learns to control this tremendous source of power, he can use it to meet any challenge and to make his greatest contribution to those around him. Here it is that I value Gandhi's example very much, because it shows that we all have the choice to undertake this transformation ourselves. This was pointed out with keen insight by the Compassionate Buddha. When people used to go to him complaining that they were upset, telling him, "Our children upset us; our partner agitates us," his simple reply would be, "You are not upset because of your children or your partner; you are upset because you are upsettable." The choice is ours to make ourselves unupsettable.

DON'T WAIT UNTIL ANGER HAS BECOME RAGE

The simple solution I would suggest to the problem of anger is repetition of the mantram. This is how we can become slow to anger and quick to forgive. Do not wait until you have developed a full-blown rage, when judgment is clouded and the mind is heaving up and down; it will be very difficult to hang on to the mantram then, or even to remember it. Try to remember the mantram as soon as you feel anger beginning to rise, when the first storm warnings are out. If possible, go out for a fast walk repeating the mantram. I need hardly add here that you are much more likely to remember the mantram at times like this if you have been using it regularly throughout your day.

RESENTMENT

Anger doesn't always appear on the stage of our consciousness with a red face and flaring nostrils; it also takes the form of resentment. Slow, burning resentments consume as much of our vital capital as outbursts of anger do, and they can just as surely poison a relationship, too. When we nurse them and dwell on them, resentments can wear a kind of groove in our consciousness. When we resent a person, for whatever reason, we find more and more things to be resentful about, and when we go on like this, this old record of resentments can be set off just by the sound of that person's voice, or even by a car the same color as theirs.

Even if you can't remember the mantram when you are angry, you can always use it when you are resentful. Instead of repeating the same old resentment over and over, substitute the holy name. I believe that it was Thomas Jefferson who said, "When you are angry, count to ten before you speak." I would say, when you are angry, repeat the mantram ten times before you speak; when you are very angry, repeat it a hundred times, and when you are resentful, just keep on repeating it as long as you can.

IMPATIENCE

Impatience is another of anger's poor relations. We can hardly wait for the other person to get out of our way so we can do what we want; we can hardly wait for him to finish his sentence so that we can speak. I still get taken aback to hear drivers honking their horns when the car ahead of them doesn't move the instant the traffic light turns green. Patience, on the other hand, is one of the most marvelous qualities in life. With patience we can bear with others despite their drawbacks; we can support them even when they make mistakes and still point out these mistakes lovingly and constructively. When we practice patience, we are responding to the real person, not to the mask of greed or anger that he or she is wearing. Patience is an unfailing remedy for friction in personal relations, and one given us long ago in the beautiful line from Proverbs, "A soft answer turneth away wrath." Even if a person has never won a beauty contest, has no money in the bank, can't even change a flat tire, if he or she has inexhaustible patience, then we will find that life with such a person will never grow stale.

When disciples used to ask the Buddha, "How do we become more patient?" he would reply, "By trying to become more patient." We don't develop patience by wishing that we were more patient, or by wearing a button which says I Am Patient; we learn patience by trying. I once asked my grandmother why there should be people to criticize me and attack me, and she replied, "How else can you learn patience?"

If we can remember the mantram, it will help us to be more patient, and our example will help the other person to be more patient too. When a flood of impatient words is rising, shut your mouth and keep saying the mantram; let the harsh words dash themselves against the back of your teeth if they have to, but don't let them out. Even if you think that you'll jump out of your skin if that car ahead doesn't leap into motion a split second after the light turns green, keep repeating the mantram. It will keep your hand off the horn and your blood pressure down, and best of all, it will transform the rising power of impatience into that most precious of qualities, patience.

GREED

Greed is another of the undesirable weeds which we can root out of our consciousness through the use of the mantram. I use "greed" here to stand for selfish desire in all its varied forms: the greed for personal power, for prestige, for profit, for pleasure; the belief that we can find abiding happiness in pursuing our own selfish satisfactions regardless of the cost to those around us.

Let me stress that what I am deprecating here is not desire, but *selfish* desire. An unselfish desire to alleviate the suffering of those around us, or to contribute to the welfare of those around us, is the highest of human motivations. Mahatma Gandhi, who worked with no thought of personal power or prestige or profit, was once asked by a European reporter, "Don't you have any ambition?" He replied, "I am the most ambitious of men: I want to reduce myself to zero." In other words, he wanted to eliminate all selfish desires completely. A selfish desire for my own personal profit, for example, can be transformed into a selfless desire to see that everyone has shelter, clothing, and enough to eat; it is just a matter of spiritual engineering. So when I use the word *greed*, I am referring to selfish desire.

Action motivated by greed is not likely to be in our own best interests, or in the best interests of others, and in the end it will leave us unsatisfied and alienated. When we are driven by greed, it is as if we go through life wearing blinders which enable us to see only through a little slit. The man who is driven by greed for money, for example, looks at the world through a slit shaped like a dollar sign; when he looks at a sunny meadow all he is thinking is, "I could make a mint building a subdivision here."

BURGUNDY CHERRY ICE CREAM

We have all been conditioned to believe that by fulfilling our desires we will find lasting satisfaction. Suppose the desire for a burgundy cherry ice cream cone arises in your mind, and you go buy one and eat it. If I ask you just then, "Are you satisfied?" you will assure me that you are. But if I ask an hour later, "Does that burgundy cherry cone still bring you some satisfaction?" you will say, "That was an hour ago."

With penetrating insight, the mystics will tell us that when we have a desire for a certain thing, a certain experience, and we fulfill that desire, the happiness we feel is not something given by that thing or that experience; it is due to having no craving for a little while. It is not because this craving has been satisfied, but because for just a little while there is a state of no craving.

But the mind does not rest long in this state of no desire. The mind is a factory manufacturing desires in all makes and models and colors, working overtime seven days a week. With that first bite of burgundy cherry ice cream, you shut your eyes and let your taste buds rejoice, but by the time you are halfway through the cone, you are already thinking about a cup of coffee or the shoe sale next door.

It is the nature of a desire to exhaust itself, the mystics say. Even if eating that burgundy cherry cone gives you satisfaction – and no one is denying that – how long does this satisfaction last? More than that, if you keep on eating ice cream, cone after cone, satisfaction soon turns to satiation, and then eventually to revulsion. But this hasn't helped to get rid of the desire: when you are hungry again, the desire will be back, and no amount of indulgence on the physical level can root it out, because desire is in the mind.

DESIRES COME AND GO

There is much more satisfaction in resisting a wrong desire than in yielding to it. I once enabled a woman to give up smoking just by telling her this; she was responsive to my concern and she had the capacity to accept the challenge my words implied. A great many people would gladly quit smoking, a habit which mounting evidence on all sides shows to be extremely harmful, if they only had the will. Perhaps you have tried to give up smoking: suddenly something will remind you of tobacco and the desire for a cigarette rises in your mind. If you give in to this desire, you are not likely to succeed in giving up smoking, and when the cigarette is gone, you will be left with that shabby feeling that all your good resolves have come to naught. At times like these, use the mantram to strengthen your will. Desires are short-lived; at first the desire will loom over you like a tiger, but if you can hold out for just a little while by repeating the mantram, you will see the desire shrink to the size of a mouse and scurry out under the door. You may not have seen the last of the tiger, but after a few experiences like this, you gain confidence that the mantram *will* reduce that tiger to a mouse, and finally seal up the mouse hole in the bargain.

THE NATURE OF DESIRE

An ancient Indian scripture, the Chandogya Upanishad, gives us a penetrating insight into the nature of desire when it says, "There is no joy in the finite; there is joy only in the infinite." What we are all looking for is unending joy, a delight that never pales or cloys. But if we try to find this unending joy on the physical level, where it is the very nature of things to change, then we have lost it. I have known some very wealthy people, some famous people, some people who have indulged in all of the pleasures that life has to offer. When I have asked them very candidly whether they have found what they are looking for, they confide, if they are honest and sensitive: "What we were looking for seems to have slipped through our fingers."

I have observed that young people today are remarkably free from greed for power and profit, but they make up for this in the great faith they put in pleasure. The pursuit of pleasure has become a cult today, and not only with the young. This is partly our deep belief that in gratifying our senses we can become beautiful and fulfilled, and partly our wrong conditioning by the mass media, which is now in the very air we breathe. Today, the pursuit of pleasure causes more unhappiness and more broken relationships than we are prepared to admit.

Sex, for example, cannot be viewed as simply a source of pleasure without many unfortunate consequences. The sex drive is a tremendously powerful force. On the physical level it brings two people together; on the spiritual level, when harnessed, this same power can bring us together into union with all life. In other words, sex is sacred. It has a beautiful place in a loyal and loving relationship. But when a relationship is based entirely on the physical level, on physical appeal, that appeal will eventually exhaust itself.

It is a law just like Newton's law of gravity. If a relationship is not founded on mutual love and respect – and let me point out that we have to work at this day by day by putting the needs of the other person before our own – then when the physical appeal goes, the relationship *has* to fall apart. The tendency here is to blame the other person, or to say, "Oh, well, I guess it just didn't work out." When we do this, we go through life never suspecting that we cannot build a lasting relationship on the physical level, and we find ourselves enacting the same drama over and over.

Desire is in the mind. The man or woman who gains some mastery over the thinking process finds that the senses have become faithful servants. This is not bleaching the color out of life; it is gaining mastery over life.

DESIRES DRIVE US INTO ACTION

From my university teaching days, I recall an incident which illustrates how desire can drive us to action. I had a colleague in the physics department who was completely devoted to research work. He was never without his coffee, from which I gathered that coffee and research work go together. In fact, he was always in his chair with his journals and his slide rule; he never used to go for walks, and I had seldom seen him very active. One night, when I was coming back after a late show a mile from the campus, I saw him walking by the movie theater. I was astonished; I thought he had forgotten how to walk. "What made you throw yourself out of your chair and walk all this way?" I asked him. "You're breaking the habits of a lifetime." "Coffee," he muttered. "I ran out of coffee. I knew I could get some near here even at this hour." So I asked, "Why didn't you just stay at your desk and keep working?" "I couldn't concentrate," he said. "No matter what I read, all I could think about was coffee. Thermodynamics turned into coffee; Planck's constant turned into coffee; everything turned into coffee. I just had to get some."

This is the power that is locked up in our desires. If just this little desire for a cup of coffee – not exactly the strongest of our addictions – can have so much power, how much more power must there be in a stronger desire? Of course, I took advantage of the occasion to tell my friend that that is the time to repeat the mantram, because when you have a powerful urge, it acts like a hammer: *coffee, coffee, coffee.* If you can change *coffee, coffee, coffee* to *Rama, Rama, Rama* or *Jesus, Jesus, Jesus,* that same power will be used to drive the holy name into your consciousness. This is true for all negative emotions. Fear is a hammer; anger is a sledge hammer; and any self-centered desire is a real pile driver.

THE JOURNEY

Desire is power which we can harness or let go to waste. We have all been given this power for one purpose: to realize the indivisible unity of life; as the Buddha would put it, to cross from this shore of separateness to the far shore of unity. It is a little like crossing from Berkeley to San Francisco. Some people drive straight to the freeway and over the bridge to the other shore. Other people are like those trucks you see with the words Frequent Stops on the back: they stop for a pizza, they stop to see what is on sale at the Co-op, they stop to see what an old friend is up to. Such people will never make it to the freeway; they won't reach the other shore before night comes. Now, we all have a certain margin of error for making a few stops. Experimenting with the toys of life and finding that they don't fully satisfy us is part of growing up. But when we keep on making stops all our life, it is tragic. Then, even if after many years we get a glimpse of the purpose of life, we may not have the fuel left to make the journey.

So don't waste the precious power of desire to make little trips to the local shopping mall, or short excursions to the restaurant, the bowling alley, the video store. Make a few trips to these spots, and then learn that there is not much doing at these local destinations. Begin conserving your energies to undertake the really big adventure we were all born for. Don't postpone a day.

CHAPTER NINE

The Mantram at the Time of Death

THROUGHOUT OUR VILLAGE my grandmother was looked up to as a source of great strength; so when death was approaching, people used to send for her to sit beside them and comfort them in their last hours. Sometimes she would insist that I accompany her, even when I was still a child. As I sat by the side of the dying while my grandmother held their hand, the sorrow and the agony I witnessed used to torture me. In those days, I didn't understand why she took me to these terrible scenes, but their impact on my consciousness was profound. The question began to haunt me, "Is this going to happen to me too? Is there no way I can go beyond death?"

Every morning my grandmother used to go to our ancestral temple for worship. On her return, she would stick behind my ear a flower offered to the Lord in worship and bless me with these simple words: "May you be like Markandeya!" Markandeya was a boy in the Hindu scriptures whose heart was filled even from childhood with love for God. When death came to claim him in his sixteenth year, he sat down in deep meditation on God, one of whose names in Sanskrit is

Mrityunjaya, the Conqueror of Death. Realizing in the depths of his consciousness his unity with the Lord, Markandeya passed beyond the sway of death. This is a story familiar to every Hindu boy, so when I heard my grandmother tell me every morning "May you be like Markandeya," it sank very deep into me. By this constant reminder and by taking me to those scenes of grief beside the dying, she made me aware of death and gave me the intense desire to go beyond it. More than that, she showed me that death could be transcended in this very life.

THE SIGNIFICANCE OF DEATH

Everyone will agree that some day the body must grow old, decay, and drop away, but not many will face the fact that it will happen to them. The proof is that if a person really believes he will die, he will do something about it. If I may say so, very few understand the real significance of death. Those who realize that the purpose of death is to go beyond death can use death itself to do this. When we know fully that we are not this changing body but the changeless Self who dwells in the body, we conquer death here and now.

We hear a great deal about death these days; everywhere we look there are books and seminars on dying. This is a change for the better, because until recently death has been a forbidden topic in our society. When we draw a curtain around death, hiding it away out of sight in hospitals and rest homes, our lives can become shallow. But talking about death is only a first step. These books and seminars are intended to help us to accept death, but they do not show us how to go beyond it.

Talking about death can be a real service if it enables people to shed the body more peacefully or more courageously, but the mantram can do this for us far more effectively than any intellectual discussion.

THE MANTRAM AT THE MOMENT OF DEATH

In India, as in other traditions, it is the custom to sing the mantram beside a dying person. This helps to console the family, as well as the person who is about to die. But it is even more effective for the person who is dying to repeat the mantram silently, in the mind. The mantram can replace fear and confusion with the calm atmosphere so important at this great transition.

All the mystics tell us to live each moment as if it were our last, and the man or woman who repeats the mantram regularly and with real devotion is actually preparing for this. The person who has become established in the mantram, who has made the mantram an integral part of his or her consciousness, is prepared for death at all times. Mahatma Gandhi, explaining this state, said once that it would be easier for his life to stop than for his mantram *Rama* to cease reverberating in his consciousness. And this is indeed how it came to pass: when his body was pierced by the assassin's bullets, Gandhi blessed his attacker with folded hands and fell with *Rama* on his lips and in his heart.

If we are able to repeat the mantram at the moment of death, the great mystics tell us, we merge into God just as a bursting bubble becomes one with the sea. This is not just a Hindu idea; we find it in all the other great religions too. I remember a friend once confiding in me how comforting he found it as a child when one of his teachers, a very loving nun, told him that he would go straight to heaven if he were saying the Hail Mary at the moment he died. We tend to forget as adults that children can often be deeply troubled by questions about death, and this boy found himself more responsive than ever to the beautiful Hail Mary because it eased his fears and gave him some sense of control over his destiny.

This idea that the mantram can be our salvation at the moment of death is not as simplistic as it may seem at first. It's not as if we can lead as selfish and sensate a life as we please until the very last second and then say the holy name and attain salvation. It is not possible to say the mantram with all our heart at the moment of death unless we have been repeating it for a long time before. An English disciple once asked his spiritual teacher, Sri Ramana Maharshi, why he couldn't just throw himself under a train repeating the mantram and attain salvation without all those years of discipline. Sri Ramana Maharshi's penetrating answer was that his last thought would not be the mantram; it would be the "I" thought.

THE PROCESS OF DEATH

The process of death as described by the great mystics may throw some light on why this is so. Dying, they tell us, is a more complicated process than we ordinarily think. It is not sudden; it is a gradual withdrawal of consciousness from the body into the Self. First, consciousness is withdrawn from the

senses to the mind. The senses shut down, and outer awareness of the body and of our surroundings is gone. We still have
ears, but we hear nothing because consciousness has been
withdrawn; we still have eyes, but there is nothing outside that
we see. Yet even though we can no longer see or hear, there is
still consciousness in the mind, with all its desires and regrets,
all its conflicts and hopes and fears. As long as we have these
selfish desires, conflicts, and reservations, they will remain in
the mind at a deep level, where all desires and conflicts merge
in the "I" thought at the time of death.

This process is strikingly parallel to what happens in deep
meditation. When we are concentrating deeply, we will not
hear the planes in the sky or the cars on the road, because we
have withdrawn consciousness from the senses. The crucial
difference is that in meditation this is a voluntary withdrawal,
whereas in death it is involuntary. In meditation, however, we
go even further: we deliberately seek to withdraw consciousness not only from the senses, but from the mind as well. This
is what stilling the mind means.

To withdraw consciousness from the senses into the mind
is not too hard, but it is very difficult to withdraw consciousness at will from the mind into the Self, into the core of purity
and perfection which is at the very center of our being. Yet as
long as the mind has not been stilled through the practice of
meditation and the repetition of the mantram, consciousness
will remain in the mind at the moment of death. We will still
be identified with the ego, and our last thought will be *I, I, I*. To
repeat the mantram at this stage is impossible if we have only

been saying it on the surface level of consciousness, for there is no surface level any longer. To be able to repeat the mantram at the actual moment of death, the mantram must have sunk very, very deep into the mind – so deep that instead of our last thought being *I, I, I,* the last thought will be of God, whose symbol is the mantram.

This has tremendous practical significance. If we have been living for ourselves, our last thought will be of ourselves, and there will be no way to avoid the suffering of ego-identification when the body is wrenched away. Abruptly, everything that we hold dear will be snatched away from us: our possessions, our cherished plans for the future, our loved ones, and even our body and the miscellaneous collection of likes and dislikes, habits and opinions that we are pleased to call our personality. Unless we have worked long and hard to cultivate detachment from all this – in other words, unless we have been trying to lead the spiritual life – the pain of this separation will be terrible. But if we have been repeating the mantram with sincerity and enthusiasm until it has become an integral part of our consciousness, even in life we can always be completely mindful of the deathless, changeless reality we call God. Then, when the body is shed, our individual consciousness will merge in the Lord, who is our real and deepest Self.

In other words, even in life, the person who has realized the indivisible unity of life has already died to all that was separate in him, all that was selfish in her, to come to life in the Lord. This is why Saint Francis says, "It is in dying that we are born to eternal life." This death of the ego is the purpose of all the disciplines of the spiritual life. Even in little things, whenever we are very patient or cheerfully do something we dislike, a little of our selfishness and self-will has died. Little by little we surrender everything – not under duress, but entirely by free choice, until we no longer need to hang on to anything outside us for support. Then, once we are established in this state of unity, we are established in it forever. This is what Jesus means when he offers us life everlasting: our constant awareness of the unity of life, our constant awareness of God, is not interrupted even when the physical body dies.

THE BODY IS A JACKET

My grandmother, who was not intellectually oriented, had a rather different but very vivid way of getting this point across. I remember once asking her why death should involve so much suffering. She didn't answer directly; she just told me to go sit in a big wooden chair there in our ancestral home. "You hold on to this chair as hard as you can," she said, "I'm going to try to pull you out." I held on to the chair with all my might, and she began to pull. She was a strong woman, and when she started to pull I thought my arms were going to come off, but I held on for all I was worth. Finally, despite all my resistance, she wrenched me out of the chair. "That hurt, Granny," I said. "Let's try it again," she replied, "but this time don't hold on." I didn't, and there was no struggle, no pain; she raised me effortlessly and gracefully into her arms.

It was a very eloquent answer. Death is going to take our body anyway, no matter what we do, and the more we try to hang on to the body with all its desires and fears, the more we are going to suffer when death wrenches these things away. On the other hand, when we overcome identification with the body and ego through meditation and the repetition of the mantram, we know from direct spiritual experience that the body is not us, but only a jacket which we have been wearing all these years. Then, when the jacket has become worn and can no longer serve us, we do not cry because it has gone the way of all jackets; we simply take it off, hang it up carefully, and go home.

REINCARNATION

Perhaps it would not be out of place here to mention reincarnation, as it is interpreted in Eastern mysticism. The Hindu and Buddhist scriptures tell us that when consciousness is consolidated at the moment of death, our last thought will encompass our entire life. At that instant, all the desires of our lifetime are consolidated in one deep, driving desire, which determines our destiny. It is this desire which impels us to take a body again, so that our desires may be satisfied.

According to this presentation, we are reborn into a context that is ideally suited for us to work on our weak points. If our last thoughts are of ourselves, we will be reborn into a family and environment just right for showing us that by living for ourselves we can never find fulfillment. But if we have learned to live not for ourselves but for others, then when we die we no longer have any personal desires to fulfill, and we merge quietly and peacefully into God. We have already been united with him in our lifetime, and when it falls away, the body no more disturbs this unity than a falling leaf disturbs the tree.

The mystics of Hinduism and Buddhism have a very expressive way of presenting this. They tell us that this world is like an immense school, where we have all been enrolled in order to learn that all life is one. This is the supreme goal of life, and our only reason for being here on earth is to discover this unity for ourselves. When we do this, the Lord says, "Very good; you've graduated. Now you don't have to go to school any more." But if at the end of our life we still have not made this discovery, the Lord tells us very compassionately, "I think you'd better come back next semester and work a little harder."

I have heard that W. C. Fields wanted his epitaph to read, "On the whole, I'd rather be in Philadelphia." If that *was* his last wish, he may well be there now, disguised as someone else. In other words, whatever context we find ourselves in in this life, this is a choice which we have made ourselves. And the very positive aspect of this concept of reincarnation is that it places the responsibility for our spiritual evolution squarely on our own shoulders. We cannot complain that our society has molded us, that our parents have influenced us, and then sit back and say, "There is nothing I can do to change myself." There is everything that we can do. We got ourselves into the situation we are in, and we can get ourselves out once we begin to make the right choices in life.

In this way of looking at things, none of us is lost. We are all working towards the discovery of the unity of life, however long it may take. Our present life is a fresh opportunity to move closer to the supreme goal, and the choice is entirely ours whether or not we make the best use of this opportunity. This is a very practical, positive conclusion, and in fact reincarnation does such a good job of explaining the human condition that it is very difficult to question it, even intellectually. But I always emphasize that when it comes to making wise choices in life, it makes not the slightest difference whether we believe in reincarnation or not. No matter how many lives we believe in, death poses the same challenge to us all. It is possible to believe in a thousand lifetimes and still lead a selfish life, and it is possible to believe in only one lifetime and still learn to become established in the mantram and realize for ourselves the supreme goal of life.

Whether or not we believe in reincarnation, whether or not we even believe that life has a goal, the mantram can be of enormous value at the hour of death. Any remembrance of the holy name is a solace that can help us to undergo the last great change called death with peace and courage in our hearts.

CHAPTER TEN

The Goal of Life

TWENTY-FIVE HUNDRED YEARS ago, ordinary people like you and me used to gather around the Compassionate Buddha, dazzled by the radiance of his personality, and ask, "Are you a god?" The Buddha would answer quietly, "No, I am awake." This is the literal meaning of the word *buddha*, "he who has awakened" – awakened from the nightmare of separate living into the light of unity.

This awakening is the highest goal of life, and though different religions call it by different names, the goal is one and the same. It is nirvana to the Buddhist, moksha to the Hindu; Christian mystics call it beautifully "entering the kingdom of heaven within." To the Sufis it is union with the Beloved; to Jewish mystics it is the return of the soul to its divine source. Sometimes it is called Christ-consciousness or Krishna-consciousness, enlightenment, illumination, or Self-realization. But there is no difference between any of these, as we can see when we keep our eyes on the goal itself rather than on the innumerable differences in rites and rituals and dogmas. No matter what they call it, all the great religions point to the same supreme goal.

THE NEED FOR AN OVERRIDING GOAL

Every one of us has an aching need for a goal worthy of our complete dedication, for an ideal so lofty that we can keep our eyes on it no matter what circumstances come our way. Much of our boredom and restlessness comes from not having a direction in life; we are like someone all dressed up on a Saturday night with nowhere to go. If I may say so, most of what we call goals are not real goals at all, because they give us no all-encompassing sense of purpose in life. But when we have an overriding goal, we find that many of our problems fall away of their own accord. Everything falls into perspective: we know what to do with our time, what to do with our energy, and it is easier to see all the little choices that confront us every day. Shall I eat what appeals to the taste buds, or what conduces to sound health? Shall I spend time doing my own thing, or doing work which benefits all those around me? Shall I move away from people just because their ways are not my ways, or shall I try to live in harmony with everyone around me? When we have our eyes on the goal of life we see these choices everywhere, all the time, and we begin to cultivate the will and wisdom to make the choices which will help us to grow to our full stature. Thus we gradually wake up to our true nature, which is ever pure, ever perfect.

At present, however, most of us are far from having this supreme goal always in sight. The vast majority of us are obsessively identified with our body, our emotions, our intellect, and our ego. We have come to believe that we are separate individuals whose fulfillment lies in seeking our own satisfaction, even at the expense of those around us.

In traditional circles we hear a good deal about heaven and hell, and many people say they do not believe in them. But heaven and hell are not places; they are states of consciousness. Hell is not a bit of overheated subterranean real estate where devils dance about with pitchforks; it is what we experience whenever we are plagued by worry or anger or jealousy or greed. Hell is the increasing loneliness and frustration we feel when we try to live for ourselves as separate individuals. And heaven, too, is a state of consciousness, which we can all enjoy right in this very life when we no longer see ourselves as separate. When we overcome our identification with the body, the mind, and the ego, we are living in freedom. When we come to see that our fulfillment lies in making the greatest possible contribution to our family, our society, and our world, we are living in harmony with the unity of life. This is living in joy; this is heaven here and now.

THE WORLD OF SEPARATENESS

In the Judeo-Christian tradition, the monstrous superstition that we are all separate is symbolized by the Fall; in the Hindu and Buddhist tradition it is called *maya*. *Maya* is a term we often hear now in the West, where it is usually translated as illusion. Literally, however, *maya* means "that which can be measured." Maya is the finite world which we perceive with the senses and grasp with the intellect; it is the world of change that is subject to death and decay. When we identify with the body, mind, and ego, with the set of habits that we are pleased to call our personality, we are wrongly identifying with maya. And as long as we are under the hypnotic spell of maya – which I like to think is connected with the word *magic* – we will go on believing that we can find lasting fulfillment in sensory pleasures, in amassing money, in acquiring great learning, in imposing our self-will on those around us.

But whatever temporary satisfaction these pursuits may give us, they cannot bring us the abiding joy that we are all seeking. Saint Augustine brings this point home when he cries out: "Lord, how can I ever find rest anywhere else when I am made to rest in thee?" What we are all looking for, even though we may be searching in the most improbable places, is infinite wisdom, infinite joy, infinite love. And this is our real nature. At the very core of our being is a spark of purity, of perfection, of divinity, because the Lord is enshrined in the heart of each of us. When we learn to identify less and less with that which is subject to change and more and more with this core of perfection, we are gradually waking up to our true nature.

THE AWAKENING

This awakening, as the Compassionate Buddha would say, is something each of us must do for himself or herself. When people would come to the Buddha and say, "Blessed One, please tell us all about this nirvana that you speak of," he would smile and reply, "Learn to meditate, so that you may find out for yourself." In other words, realizing the unity of life is not an intellectual understanding; it is an experiential discovery. It is impossible to convey in words what awareness of the unity of life is like, what it is like to have attained the highest goal that life has to offer. Shankara, the great mystic from my old state of Kerala, tells us that words and thoughts turn back frightened when they try to approach the ultimate reality. It is not measurable, so how can thoughts grasp it or words define it? Even the most inspired mystics, in the most inspired language, can only hint at it; they use words to pique our curiosity and to rouse our enthusiasm to have this experience ourselves. As Sri Ramakrishna tells us, when you have eaten a mango, you know what mangoes taste like; if you have not, the description will not mean much unless you resolve to go out and taste one for yourself.

But although the ultimate reality cannot be grasped by words or thoughts, the great mystics often go on to tell us what realization of this goal means in practical terms, what effect it has on daily living. Realization is experiential; it has a profound impact on our conduct, character, and consciousness. In the homely language of Sri Ramakrishna, when a man has eaten garlic, every breath that comes out of him will smell of garlic. When a man or woman has realized the indivisible unity of life, then everything he does, every word she utters, will be an expression of this unity. This is the infallible test of spiritual experience. You may have a bumper sticker that says All Life Is One, but if you do not have some measure of control over your thinking process, if you cannot drop a job at will or juggle with your likes and dislikes, if you cannot bear patiently with those who oppose you, then you have not yet realized the unity of life for yourself.

DETACHMENT

People usually smile and nod in approval when I say that we can come to identify more and more with the spark of divinity in all of us. But when I say that we must identify less with the body, the mind, and the ego, they begin to shift uneasily in their seats, and when I mention detachment, which is absolutely necessary for attaining the goal of life, they sometimes get up and tiptoe out the back door. The word *detachment* often strikes a negative note, but detachment is really a marvelous quality; it is the key to intentional living. Detachment does not mean that we are indifferent or unconcerned, but that we are not entangled. Detachment from work, for instance, doesn't mean that we lean back with our feet up on our desk. We work harder than ever; we do our very best, but we are not caught in the results. We don't worry about the job, and we don't get elated if we get the results we wanted or depressed if we do not. If I may say so, it is the detached worker who does the best job. Such people can put their work in a larger perspective and do it with objectivity and concentration. And in personal relations, detachment is invaluable. Only when we are detached can we really see the needs of the other person; we can respect his opinions and not get agitated by his shortcomings.

When we cease to identify ourselves with the body, we come

to see it for what it is: a very useful instrument of service. As my grandmother used to tell me, "Son, the Lord gave you these two hands not to strike at others, but to wipe away their tears." We use the body wisely like any other tool; in fact, I am fond of comparing the body to a compact car. We take good care of it by keeping it clean and giving it nourishing food in temperate quantities, and we keep it in good running order by giving it plenty of exercise. But we should never forget that we are the driver; our senses should obey us just the way well-trained horses respond to the slightest touch on the reins. When the palate clamors for something sweet but not very healthy, we should be able to say, "That's not so good for you," and the palate should reply, "Yes, boss; I won't ask again."

When we have lost our identification with the body, we no longer identify others with their bodies either. This means that we will not try to base a relationship just on physical appeal, and we will be incapable of discriminating against others on the basis of race or color. Loss of body-consciousness does not mean that we go around bumping into things, but that we no longer try to base our security on the body. This gives us a good deal of immunity to disease, especially psychosomatic ailments; it gives us abundant vitality throughout our life and leaves us unperturbed by the ravages of time on the body.

When we cease to identify ourselves with the mind, we come to see it, too, as a very useful instrument. It is our internal instrument, just as the body is the external instrument. The mind is adept at pulling things apart, looking for cause and effect, labeling and classifying. I am not deprecating the well-trained intellect; it is quite useful in solving certain kinds of problems, such as how to get water from the well to the house or how to land a man on the moon. But intellectual knowledge alone will not get us very far in life. You may know all about quantum physics, but this is of very little use when you are in emotional turmoil. You may have written an article on the word *forgiveness* in the New Testament, but can you remain unagitated when someone criticizes your article? Sri Ramakrishna calls intellectual knowledge "rice-and-banana knowledge": it is useful for buying our food, sometimes for getting things done, but it doesn't really help us to live. We must be able to put what we know into practice for the art of living.

When we do not identify ourselves with the mind, we keep our minds open and youthful. Our likes and dislikes are held lightly, and we can juggle with them just as a trained juggler juggles with those colored balls. We enjoy things we like; we enjoy things we used not to like if they benefit those around us; we can drop a job at will. We can throw a pet opinion out into the arena and let everybody trample on it while we look on in detached interest. If the opinion is damaged, we discard it; if it is still intact, we keep it, and often those who just danced on this very same opinion will say, "That is a good opinion; we would like to share it with you." And if a resentful thought happens to rise in our mind, we do not get agitated and say, "I am resentful"; we just watch that little resentful thought sail out of sight into the distance. It is only when we identify with our thoughts and dwell on them that this stray wisp of resentfulness can billow up and cover the sky like a dark monsoon cloud. With increasing detachment from our thoughts, we find the mind becoming less and less subject to ups and downs, vacillations, and oscillations; our concentration improves, and we are able to accomplish a great deal of work without tension and without fatigue.

At last, when we cease to identify with the ego, we are no longer looking at life through our own needs and prejudices; we see life whole.

EGO

At present, most of us see ourselves as a separate fragment in a world of fragments. We are looking at life through the little keyhole of our own ego, and of course our view is very narrow, very limited, very disoriented. We think of ourselves first; "look out for number one" is an apt motto for the ego. "How will this situation affect me?" the ego asks. "How can I manipulate that person to my benefit; how can I grab as much as I can and give as little as I can?"

People who identify strongly with the ego tend to have a great deal of self-will. In fact, a good working definition of self-will is the drive to have one's own way, which comes from an intense preoccupation with one's own needs, desires, and aims. In our modern way of life, self-will is not always seen as an impediment to personal fulfillment, but is even encouraged as a good quality. It is in our relations with other people that we can most easily see the damaging effects of self-will. It is my observation that it is because we cultivate self-will in our modern approach to life that we find personal relationships, which should be a source of joy and fulfillment, difficult and even painful.

I am always reminded of this when I see those huge trailers on the freeway with the little red sign at the back: Caution – Wide Load. These vehicles take up all of their own lane and some of the lanes on either side too. On smaller roads, other vehicles can barely get by them, and oncoming cars practically have to drive into the ditch. People with a wide load of self-will go through life like this; they should have that little red sign at the back too: Wide Load. They are insensitive to the needs of others; they try to impose their self-will on those around them and shove other people out of the way without even realizing what they are doing. It is only natural in life that such people are disliked and avoided, and end up more and more lonely and insecure.

When we are locked into ourselves through compulsive identification with the ego, it is very much like being in prison. The greater our identification with the ego, the higher and stronger are the walls of our private Bastilles. When we see life whole, we are no longer looking at the world through that little keyhole; we have enlarged the keyhole, then removed the door, and finally even demolished the prison walls. Then we are naturally sensitive to other people's needs, other people's points of view. We are able to help them effectively, and we become incapable of blaming them or holding the past against them. We come to see that in exploiting others we are working to the detriment of all, and we can forgo our own satisfactions gladly if this will contribute to the welfare of our family, our friends, and our society. We come to see the joy of others as our joy and their suffering as our suffering, and we have the will and wisdom to help alleviate this suffering and contribute to their joy.

This, of course, is a complete change in our usual perspective. To see the whole we have to turn our back on the ego; to see the unity we have to turn our back on separateness. As we begin to change our perspective in this way and come to see the indivisible unity of life, we will be amazed to see that we had always been looking at life upside down. Sometimes the scriptures and great mystics of all religions resort to seemingly paradoxical language to put this point across. Jesus tells us, "He who would seek to find himself shall lose himself, and he who loses himself shall find himself"; the person who overcomes identification with the limited ego will find the source of abiding joy and limitless love which is our real nature. As Saint Paul exclaims after becoming united with Christ, "Not I, not I, but Christ liveth in me."

But we do not turn our back on the ego overnight. We do not go to bed one night as a feverish fragment of ego-consciousness and wake up the next morning in blissful awareness of unity. This is not something that can be done by taking a pill or attending a weekend seminar, by reading books or plugging ourselves into alpha-wave machines. It takes years of sustained effort, and it is anything but easy. There is a good deal of pain in going against self-will. You may feel that you have got to do as the ego dictates or you will die, and in a sense this is just what is happening. Each time you go against self-will, in little ways like remembering the needs of your family before your own or not postponing a disagreeable job, the ego shrinks just a little; the barrier between you and the Lord falls just a little. This is what the mystics call dying to self. Over a long, long time the separate ego dies completely, and we come to life in the Lord; we realize our unity with the One who is enshrined in the very depths of our consciousness. In the words of Meister Eckhart, a great German mystic, "The old man dies and the new man is born; the pauper dies and the prince is born."

When we are full of ourselves, we leave the prince no room to enter our lives, but as we gradually empty ourselves of all that is selfish and separate in us, God can fill us with himself. In the Hindu tradition, there is a story in which the Lord, represented as Krishna, was playing on his flute while Radha, who stands for the human soul longing for union with the divine, watched with her eyes full of envy. "What has your flute done to enjoy the blessing of being held up to your lips hour after hour?" she asked. Krishna took the flute from his lips and held it so that Radha could see inside. "Look, it's completely empty," he said, "so I can fill it with my divine melody."

The Bhagavad Gita tells us that we have only one enemy in the world: our will, and only one friend in the world: our will. When we let self-will propel us to seek our own private satisfactions at the expense of those around us, then our will really is our own worst enemy, because it is alienating us from the source of abiding joy and unshakable security within us. On the other hand, when we turn our will against the ego, taking advantage of the innumerable little opportunities throughout the day to reduce self-will, then the will is helping us to grow to our full stature.

EFFORT AND GRACE

For the vast majority of us, our will is operative only on the surface level of consciousness. We have no say in what goes on deeper in consciousness, where most of our problems have their roots. But we can learn to deepen our will, to strengthen it immeasurably. You must have seen weight-lifters showing off their biceps on Muscle Beach – in my mother tongue we call this "making frogs leap under the skin." Strengthening the will is very much like developing our muscles: an unused will atrophies, and a will that is exercised regularly grows. When Jesus teaches us to pray, "Thy will be done," he is reminding us that in exercising our will to overcome our separateness and selfishness, we are remaking ourselves into instruments of the divine will.

Meister Eckhart tells us in vivid language why sustained effort is necessary to effect this transformation. He says that we all have the seed of God within us, just as pears have pear seeds and apples have apple seeds. But the wise gardener doesn't expect a tree laden with ripe apples to appear by magic. He plants the seed in the proper soil, waters it and weeds around it, and then protects the young tree for many years and prunes it carefully, so that it will bear good fruit. Similarly, the God-seed is waiting to germinate in the depths of our consciousness, but we must all cultivate our potential for spiritual awareness by sustained and systematic effort. And as Gandhi tells us, full effort is full victory.

Yet, though we must put forth all our effort, I have no hesitation in saying that ultimately it is the grace of God that sets us free. We have to practice meditation regularly and systematically, repeat the mantram at every opportunity, and make every effort to reduce our self-will by observing all the other spiritual disciplines too, but we cannot attain the goal by human effort alone. From any genuine mystic in any religious tradition, you will hear the same note of awe and wonder: how did I, so weak, so full of shortcomings, succeed in overcoming all these immense obstacles?

In the early days, grace may come to us as the desire to overcome desire – the desire to have some mastery over our thinking process. For a long time in life we take it for granted that we must be buffeted about by self-centered desires and cravings, at the mercy of the senses and the mind. But finally we get tired of being buffeted about, and it slowly dawns on us that we could have some say in what goes on in consciousness. One of my friends tells me that he was once walking along just after turning in a term paper that he had been working on for days. "I'm a free man now," he said, but all sorts of miscellaneous thoughts about things he ought to have put into the paper kept tumbling through his mind. "I don't have to stand for this," he thought, and it occurred to him to repeat *Om* in the back of his mind. He didn't know exactly what *Om* meant, but he had heard of it as a sacred formula, and it seemed better to repeat that than to keep thinking about a paper that had already been turned in. That, of course, is exactly what the mantram is for, and it laid to rest all those other thoughts that had been nagging him. This is the rising desire to have some control over consciousness, and a few months later this friend took to the practice of meditation after hearing me present the spiritual life as the path that leads to freedom.

The desire to go beyond desire is the longing for freedom rising from deep within us. In the language of Sri Ramakrishna, the Divine Mother has looked upon us from the corner of her beautiful eyes, filled with love for us. When that glance falls on us, there comes the desire to be free, and the will to practice the disciplines which will set us free.

Grace may come to us in many unsuspected forms in the early days. For some it comes as a deep restlessness, which arises from being dissatisfied with living life on the surface level of consciousness. Often this shows up as dissatisfaction with our old pursuits, or the quality of our living, or our personal relationships, or even with ourselves. Many times people have confessed to me, "I just don't like myself," and I take this as a very promising sign. Why should we be satisfied with ourselves as we are now, when we have vastly greater reserves of strength and wisdom within us?

At first we may try to relieve this restlessness by switching jobs, or changing lifestyles, or traveling to distant places. Eventually, however, we see that nothing can satisfy us except turning inward and mastering ourselves. If any of this kind of dissatisfaction leads us to turn inward and take up the practice of the spiritual life, that is a sure sign of grace.

Often restlessness drives us into all sorts of adventures, in which we keep seeking new challenges to pit ourselves against. No sooner have we met one challenge than we need a bigger one. This is what motivates many mountain climbers, for example. Climbing is arduous and dangerous, and the challenge and the concentration and commitment it requires change all its hardships into joy. So even looking for adventure may be the call from within. In setting out to cross the sea of the mind, you will find a lifelong challenge which will test every ounce of your endurance.

In the early days, when grace first touches us, we often don't understand it; we may even struggle against it. As we become more and more restless, more and more dissatisfied with life on the surface level of consciousness, we may throw ourselves even more recklessly into the pursuit of pleasure or profit. As Meister Eckhart puts it, we thrash about like a fish caught by the divine fisherman's hook. The hook has entered the fish's flesh, and as it struggles to get free, the hook only goes in deeper and deeper. We fling ourselves with redoubled zeal into our old pursuits, hoping to get the same old satisfaction from them; but the more we try, the less satisfaction we find and the more frustrated we become. Only after a long time does it finally dawn on us that we may be beginning to get free. This is the touch of divine grace.

But grace is not a matter of letting some higher power do

all the work for us. In order to make progress on the spiritual path, we need to have the grace of our own mind as well. We need to strengthen our will and make the wise choices which will lead us closer to realizing the indivisible unity of life. In the early years, it is very much as if we are doing all the work ourselves; only near the end of the journey can we look back and see that even our own effort has been an expression of grace. A great Sufi mystic tells us that once, in a moment of despair, he cried out with all his heart: "Allah, Allah, how long I've been calling on you, and you still have not revealed yourself to me!" In the depths of his consciousness he heard the voice of God reply, "Who do you think has been making you call on me all this time?"

CHAPTER ELEVEN

The Mantram & Other Spiritual Disciplines

ONCE, THE STORY GOES, there was a sculptor in India who was famous for his statues of elephants, which were so perfect in every detail that if you saw one you would expect it to raise its trunk and trumpet. "How do you manage to carve such lifelike elephants?" people would ask. "It's very simple," the sculptor would reply. "I just find a big rock, take a hammer and some chisels, and remove everything that is not elephant."

In just the same way, you and I can make ourselves perfect by removing from our consciousness every trace of separateness and selfishness. What is left is our real Self, which is divine. I have deep appreciation for great music, great literature, and great art, but each of these expresses only one small facet of ourselves. To me, it appeals much more deeply to make our whole life a work of art, our every word and deed an expression of the unity of life. This is the highest art there is, and all the world's great religions have given us the tools we need to practice it, in a comprehensive body of spiritual disciplines of which the mantram is only one.

In different traditions, these disciplines are called by different names and expressed in different words but they are all intended to lead us to the same goal. These disciplines are timeless; they are as relevant to the human condition now as they were in India twenty-five hundred years ago or on the shores of Galilee in Jesus' time. They are undertaken not for the sake of discipline itself or because the scriptures say to, but because men and women of God everywhere have verified in their own lives that these disciplines can lead us to the supreme goal of life, which is the realization that all life is one.

This is not rhetoric. Realizing the unity of life is an experiential discovery that we can make for ourselves if we are prepared to make the effort required. But this is not something to be undertaken lightly or without guidance. Just as we would not set out to climb a mountain without first getting maps and finding an experienced guide who knows every foot of the ascent, we need an experienced spiritual teacher if we want to go to the summit of human consciousness. I have no hesitation in saying that this realization is impossible without the close guidance of a man or woman who has already discovered the unity of life in his or her own consciousness. Such a person cautions us against pitfalls and blind alleys along the way, encourages us as the challenges become greater, and inspires us by his or her personal example when we lose faith. But while the teacher is essential for guidance and support, we have to do the work for ourselves. Spiritual awareness is not something that just strikes us one day, like the apple falling on Sir Isaac Newton's head, and there is no shortcut to it such as taking drugs or using alpha-wave gadgets. It must be cultivated by the hard work of eliminating all that is selfish and separate in us, following a body of disciplines that is based on our teacher's own personal experience in realizing the unity of life.

On the strength of my own small experience, let me present a comprehensive eightfold body of spiritual disciplines which I have found extremely useful. These disciplines are suited for life in the modern world, and they can be practiced by any man or woman capable of some resolution, some endurance, and some sense of dedication. They do not require you to withdraw into a cave and roll a rock across the entrance behind you; you can follow this program while living in the world among family and friends, while studying on the campus or working at a job. If I may pay a loving tribute to my own spiritual teacher, my mother's mother, this is her real genius. I have great respect for the monastic tradition, but to lead the spiritual life, my grandmother taught me, we don't have to retire from life; we don't have to leave our family, drop out of school, or give up our job. I am irresistibly drawn to the artistry of this approach, in which we live in the midst of the world but never take our eyes off the supreme goal of life.

1. MEDITATION

Meditation comes first among spiritual disciplines. It is not a religion; it is a technique which enables us to realize for ourselves the unity of life within any of the world's great religious traditions, or even if we profess no religion at all. There is a popular misconception that meditation is making your mind a blank, or woolgathering, or letting your mind wander around some theme. Meditation is anything but these; it is a dynamic discipline in concentration which enables us to unify our consciousness completely.

Most of us live on the surface level of consciousness, our grasshopper minds jumping from one subject to another, one desire to another, one distraction to another. But as the mind is concentrated in meditation, we learn to extend our conscious control over successively deeper realms of consciousness, just as a diver learns to take deeper and deeper dives until he is able to walk about on the seabed. In the climax of meditation, on the seabed of consciousness, we realize that we are not limited by the confines of the body or mind or even of the ego; we discover for ourselves the source of abiding joy and infinite love that is our real nature.

For your meditation, memorize an inspirational passage from the scriptures and mystical literature of the world's great religions – for example, the Prayer of Saint Francis of Assisi, or the Twenty-third Psalm, or the last nineteen verses in the second chapter of the Bhagavad Gita. Choose passages which are simple and positive, and which bear the imprint of a great mystic's own personal experience. In my books *Timeless Wisdom* and *God Makes the Rivers to Flow* you will find a wide selection of pieces suitable for meditation. If you have memorized a number of such passages, that will help to avoid the possibility of the words becoming stale or mechanical. Then, with your eyes gently closed, go through the words of the passage in your mind as slowly as you can. Do not follow any association of ideas, but keep to the words of the memorized piece. When distractions come, do not resist them, but give more and more of your attention to the passage. The secret here is that we become what we meditate on; sustained concentration on the inspirational passage drives it deep into our consciousness.

This method has become known as passage meditation, and it is a perfect way to begin the day. It is good to have your meditation as early as is convenient for you, while the morning is still and cool and before the noise and bustle of the day begins. Devote half an hour each morning to the practice of meditation; do not increase this half-hour period, but if you want to meditate more, have half an hour in the evening also.

In addition to a fixed time, it is also good to have a fixed place for meditation – if not a room, at least a special corner. It should be quiet, cool, clean, and well ventilated. Keep that room for meditation, the repetition of the mantram, and spiritual reading only; do not use it for any other purpose. Gradually it will become so closely associated with meditation for you that you will have only to go into that room to become a little more calm, a little more patient, a little more loving.

You may sit on the floor for your meditation or in a straight-back chair, preferably one with arms. It is not important whether you sit in the full lotus position or the half lotus or in no lotus at all; the important thing about posture is that you sit with your head, neck, and spinal column in a straight line and your eyes gently closed. As your concentration deepens, your nervous system will begin to relax and you may experience drowsiness. When this happens, draw yourself up and move away from your back support.

Under no circumstances should you skip your meditation. If necessary, get up a little earlier to be sure that you have enough time. There is a saying in India that if you skip one day's meditation, it takes seven days to catch up. A fixed time and a fixed place are a great aid to regularity in meditation, which when practiced with regularity and sustained enthusiasm can bring about a marvelous transformation of consciousness.

Very often when people think of someone seated motionless in meditation with eyes closed, they say, "Meditation is passive; meditation is turning in on yourself." Let me assure you that meditation is anything but passive. It is hard, hard work, even though the work is all being done on the inside. But the will and concentration we develop in meditation are meant to be turned outward, to be applied in our work, in our studies, in our relations with other people. It is very much like an athlete doing the broad jump. When he goes back to get a running start, the spectators don't say, "Look, he's going in the wrong direction; he's not going to jump!" They know that he is going back to get the distance he needs for a good running start, which will carry him much further than if he had just jumped from where he stood. When we turn inward in meditation, we are getting the momentum we need to leap far in our daily life. As our meditation improves, we learn to jump right over our petty likes and dislikes to do our work with concentration and detachment, passing through personal relations with graceful artistry and a minimum of friction.

2. THE MANTRAM

Next to meditation, repetition of the mantram is perhaps the most powerful of spiritual techniques when practiced as part of a comprehensive approach to spiritual living. Meditation is a discipline which requires sustained effort and will; the mantram requires neither to be effective. I like to say that repeating the mantram is like calling on God collect. You call the Lord and say, "I don't have any money, so don't send me any bills; I don't have any will, so don't ask me to undergo any disciplines," and the Lord replies with infinite patience, "Never mind; I'll pay the bill. It's enough that you even thought of me at all."

In most orthodox Hindu traditions and even by some mystics of the Roman Catholic and Eastern Orthodox churches in the West, the mantram itself is used for meditation. This is sometimes confusing to those who are following the eight-point program presented here, so I find it helpful to draw a sharp distinction between meditation and the repetition of the mantram. Meditation is a rigorous discipline, for which I have found a long inspirational passage to be most effective in our modern, intellectually oriented age. But the mantram requires no discipline; you may repeat it at virtually any time and in any place. If your mind wanders from the mantram, if you forget it altogether, there is no cause for regret. But the more often you remember the mantram, particularly in situations where you need to strengthen your will, the deeper it will sink into your consciousness and the greater will be the benefit you derive from repeating it.

3. SLOWING DOWN

Slowing down is a great aid to efficiency, to concentration, and to physical and emotional health. The quality of life suffers when we live under the constant pressure of time, always watching the clock and trying to make every second count. The person who can do a job fastest is not necessarily the one who can do it best. All too often when we hurry we do a shoddy job, or make mistakes which take longer to correct than if we had been slow and careful in the first place. And it is difficult to give a job our full attention when we are in a hurry. Hurry means tension and a host of physical problems which come in its wake. And hurry makes for superficial relationships, because it deprives our family and friends of our time and attention so that we are not able to be sensitive to their needs.

When I first came to this country, well-meaning friends told me, "You will be terribly shocked by the pace of life, but gradually you will adapt to it." I am happy to say that I have *not* adapted to it – not only that, but I have succeeded in slowing down a good many of my friends. But I am still grieved by the frantic pace I see around me every day. Recently I went to an ice cream parlor with a few friends, and I was amazed by the speed of both customers and waitresses. As we were going in, we saw a couple hurrying in with a little girl by the hand. The two were in a rush to get their ice cream and had forgotten that little girls have short legs and take little steps, so they were dragging her along so fast that the girl fell and skinned her knee. Inside, no sooner had we been seated than we heard a plate crashing to the floor. The waitress who took our order didn't even seem to see us, and when she banged our order down in front of us, she was gone before we could even say thank you. Far from blaming this woman, who was under a great deal of pressure, I had great sympathy for her. I would not be surprised if anyone who eats at that place gets indigestion, or if anyone who works there for long develops an ulcer; this is what hurry and pressure do to us.

In order to slow down, it is a great help to begin the day early. Get up in plenty of time for meditation and for a leisurely breakfast with your family or friends. The pace with which you begin the day is the pace you will maintain throughout the day. If you find yourself getting speeded up, repeat the mantram as a reminder to slow down. Don't try to schedule your time too rigidly, or you will only find yourself getting harried and frustrated as you inevitably fall behind schedule. It may help to eliminate some unnecessary activities from your day, if they are not part of your legitimate responsibility to family or study or work or if they do not contribute to your spiritual growth.

Your personal example of unhurried concentration will not only help you; it will help those around you too. I remember once at Christmastime waiting in a long line at the post office. I waited quietly, repeating the mantram, while the man behind me was breathing fire and brimstone down my neck – he was probably double-parked outside. After a while I turned to him and said, "I am in no hurry; why don't you take my place?" The poor chap muttered something about being caught in the rat race and relaxed visibly. The girl at the window was new at the job; she was a student working during the Christmas vacation, and she was getting more and more rattled as people pressured her to weigh their packages and give them their change faster and faster. So to her, too, I said, "You take your time; I am in no hurry." It helped her greatly. But we don't have to tell people that we are not in a hurry; we communicate it through our example of patience, concentration, and consideration for others, and everyone around us benefits.

4. ONE-POINTED ATTENTION

One-pointed attention is the mark of the person who is able to make a real contribution to any field he studies, to any task she tries her hand at. But in the modern world we have become so accustomed to dividing our attention that we take it for granted: we eat popcorn while watching a movie, we smoke while reading the paper, and we listen to music while we work or study. On the Berkeley campus, I have seen students in the cafeteria reading the *Daily Californian* with one eye and watching passersby with the other, while listening to background music, drinking a cup of coffee, and smoking a cigarette, all at the same time. Their attention is scattered in five directions.

When we divide our attention this way, we cannot do full justice to any of the things we are attending to: we do not really taste the popcorn, and we do not really see the whole movie, either. I would say that anything that is worth doing is worth giving our full attention to. Just as sunlight concentrated by a magnifying glass is able to set paper afire, one-pointed concentration on your work or studies will improve efficiency, eliminate tension, and banish boredom. And one-pointedness during the day is a tremendous aid to concentration in any field, on any subject.

When we are able to give our one-pointed attention to everything we do, other people cannot help responding deeply, no matter what the relationship: man and woman, parent and child, teacher and student, friend and friend. When we are talking to someone, for example, we should be able to give our full attention to the person we are talking to. If we look only at him, listen only to her, and do not think of what we will say in reply or how we can change the subject, we will not only improve our own concentration but benefit the other person as well. If Romeo is talking to Juliet, he should not take his eyes off her even if an elephant walks into the room. Children particularly thrive on this sort of attention. They are very keen observers, and they know when we are not really there. By giving them our full attention, we assure them of our love far more than when we buy them toys or send them off to the movies for the afternoon, and we are doing them a great service by setting a personal example of one-pointedness.

5. TRAINING THE SENSES

Whenever I talk about training the senses, I make a point of emphasizing that I do not mean denial of the senses, but discriminating restraint – with the accent on "discriminating." Most of us have never trained our senses to obey us; we have senses like unruly pups, yapping all night, biting our hand with their sharp little teeth, and chewing up our favorite shoes. In the case of a really big sense craving, it is more like a huge Great Dane dragging us along at the end of a leash. Indulging the senses weakens our will, makes our mind more restless, increases our identification with the body, and leaves us a prey to a host of physical ailments. I am not moralizing or being puritanical when I say this; I am being practical. It grieves me to see people smoking, drinking, overeating, not getting exercise, or keeping late hours, because I know that they are injuring themselves. So sense-training is not a grim form of self-torture; it leads to sound health, greater security, and a sense of freedom.

There is a good deal of artistry in training the senses too. The time to leave the dinner table, for instance, is not after you have eaten one piece of pie too many, but just when everything still tastes delicious and you would like to have just a little bit more. You stop of your own free will. There is a real sense of mastery in this, and an artistry that is absent in staying on at the table until you can scarcely move and a vague sense of regret has set in.

In other words, training the senses plays an invaluable role in learning to live in freedom. Mahatma Gandhi tells us on the basis of his own experience that control of the palate is an invaluable aid to control of the mind. If we can learn to go beyond our likes and dislikes in food and eat nourishing food in temperate quantities only when we are hungry, then we will have taken a big step towards keeping our mind even.

All the senses are pathways into consciousness. In Sanskrit, one of the words for eating means not only eating through the mouth but eating through all the senses. We eat ice cream through the mouth; we eat television through the eyes and ears. It all goes in and becomes part of consciousness. When people sit with their eyes glued to the screen during some sensate movie, they are having a seven-course meal. It never occurs to most of us that we could have some say over what goes into our consciousness. At present, anything can go in; we have no doorkeepers; the doors are open all the time. But we can learn to stop what goes in and check its credentials at the door: "This show will agitate me and give me nightmares, so I'm not going to let it come in; that book will make me more patient, so I will let it come in." There are choices to make every day in what we eat, what books we read, what kind of television we watch, what sort of conversations we have. It is by making wise choices in all these little matters that we become healthy, happy, secure, selfless, and beautiful; and one of the best ways to remind ourselves of this choice is to say the mantram.

6. PUTTING OTHERS FIRST

When we remember the needs of others and put their welfare before our own, we are gradually breaking out of the prison of our own separateness. When we go only after what pleases us and try to impose our self-will on those around us, we are building the walls of the ego-prison even higher. One of the reasons I put so much stress on the family is that it gives us countless opportunities throughout the day for reducing our self-will by putting others first. This is often extremely difficult in emotionally entangled relationships. Even if you have a headache and you're in a bad mood, it's not too hard to smile at the bank teller or say thank you to the salesclerk, but just see what happens when you get home. All too often we take out our irritability and frustration on those closest to us. This is the time to cultivate more patience, to stop dwelling on ourselves and think more of the needs of others. Above all, we should learn to cooperate rather than to compete – particularly in the home between man and woman, where competition pulls the family asunder. None of this need be done on a grand scale, with the whole world watching; it can be done in many little ways as we become more sensitive to the needs of others.

Putting other people first is showing your love for them, but this love expresses itself in different ways. In putting the postman first, for instance, you don't run out and throw your arms around him and tell him how wonderful he is; you put him first by addressing your letters neatly and legibly and by being sure to include the zip code. You put your children first by giving them as much of your time and attention as possible, by respecting their point of view, and by remembering always to set the sort of personal example that you would like them to follow. After all, it won't have much effect when you shake your finger at your son or daughter and say, "I don't want you to drink," if you have a cocktail glass in the other hand. You are also putting your children first if you help them not to develop too much self-will or to get too caught up in likes and dislikes; this kind of freedom is much more easily learned when we are young, and it will save them a great deal of unnecessary suffering.

If we really want to make progress on the spiritual path, there is no substitute for putting others first. It is the give-and-take of innumerable little encounters with others in our daily life that really wears off the angles and corners of the ego. Unless we reduce our self-will like this, we will simply have too wide a load of self-will to get through some of the strait and narrow gates into our deeper consciousness.

This is why I repeat everywhere that the spiritual life is best led in the midst of people. If we leave our family, give up our job, or drop out of school to go live in a cave high on the Himalayas, three days' journey from the nearest human being, we may find a certain peace of mind, but this is not the kind of peace that lasts. The trees won't offend us; the squirrels won't contradict us; our self-will will play dead because there is no one to rouse it, and we may say, "Ah, how calm and spiritual I am!" But when we come back into the midst of life, dealing with people whose ways are not our ways, we will be more agitated than ever. So let me assure you that whatever your present situation is, it is an excellent one for taking up the spiritual life.

Someone once asked me in very graphic language if putting the other person first all the time doesn't mean making yourself into a doormat. Not at all. We are not really putting others first if we connive at their mistakes, or if we let them have their way when they want to go in some wrong direction. It is a sign of great love and great maturity to be able to oppose the other person tenderly and resolutely when he or she is going in the wrong direction. When it seems necessary to say no, we should be able to say it gently and without the slightest trace of resentment or retaliation. We can all learn to disagree without being disagreeable.

7. SPIRITUAL FELLOWSHIP

We all need companionship and support when we are changing the very basis of our life. It is difficult to practice meditation and undo all our old conditioning, and here association with spiritually oriented people is a source of day-to-day support and inspiration. In your own home, it is very good if members of the family meditate together, but friends, too, can live together and base their lives on the same spiritual values. If possible, it is of especially great value to meet and draw inspiration from someone who is able to interpret the sacred scriptures and the great mystics in the light of his or her own personal experience.

8. SPIRITUAL READING

Readings in the scriptures and the great mystics of all religions can be a great source of inspiration. If you want to know more about mysticism and the real goal of religion, do not go to books about mysticism or religion; go direct to the great mystics themselves. They have left us a rich heritage of practical commentary on the scriptures, beautiful poetry, and the inspiring stories of their own personal discovery of the unity of life. These writings are meant to be read slowly and thoughtfully, a few pages at a time, so that you can reflect over what you read. It is particularly helpful to spend fifteen minutes or so in this kind of reading just before bedtime.

IS DISCIPLINE REALLY NECESSARY?

I have sometimes heard people ask whether practicing these disciplines isn't trying to buy God's love, to make a bargain with God. The Lord does not love us because we deserve it or because we have worked for it, but because God's very nature is pure love. God's love for us is infinite; it cannot be diminished or increased, but through the practice of meditation, repetition of the mantram, and observance of these other allied disciplines, we can make our love for the Lord within grow and deepen.

The Lord wants nothing more for each of us than that we should all be united with him. Even if, in our ignorance of should all be united with him. Even if, in our ignorance of this, we flounder around in life and cause suffering and confusion for ourselves and those around us, the only thing that will bring us real fulfillment is to realize in our own consciousness the indivisible unity of life. When we practice the disciplines on which the spiritual life is based, we reduce the suffering and confusion in our lives and make it easier for the Lord to draw us to himself, for the Divine Mother to draw us to herself.

As Sri Ramakrishna said, the grace of God is a wind which is always blowing. All that you and I have to do is to put up our sails and let this wind carry us across the sea of life to the far shore, to the "peace that passeth all understanding." But most of us are firmly stuck on this shore. Our sail is in tatters and our boat cannot even move because of all the excess baggage weighing it down. It has taken us a lifetime to collect this baggage: all our likes and dislikes, our habits and opinions; all the resentments and hostilities which we have carefully nursed, all the things we are compulsively attached to. But through the systematic practice of spiritual disciplines, we gradually toss this excess baggage overboard, patch up our sail, and unfurl it to catch the wind that will carry us to the far shore. The wind is always blowing, but we have to do the work of making our boat seaworthy. This is why I seldom speak of divine grace to people. I talk about effort, because we have to put forth all our effort before grace will be forthcoming.

There is a saying in India that when we take one step towards God, he takes seven steps towards us. The Lord is very eager to see us take the first step, but he knows us very well by now, and he watches carefully to see that we take that step and don't wobble back and forth. It is not enough just to put your foot forward or even to touch it lightly to the ground; we must put our weight on it completely. When we do take a sincere step towards the Lord, by bearing patiently with those around us, or changing some unhealthy habits, or repeating the holy name, we can be sure that the Lord will take seven steps towards us. But we must take the first step.

INTERRELATIONSHIP OF SPIRITUAL DISCIPLINES

This body of spiritual disciplines that I recommend is a total way of life. It is not meant to be practiced just one day a week or only when we feel like it; it can be followed everywhere, throughout the day, in every aspect of daily life – in the home, on the campus, at work, and even in recreation. All these disciplines go together: when you work on one of them, it strengthens you in the others, and if you neglect one of them, it affects all of them adversely. Slowing down, for instance, helps in putting others first and in developing one-pointedness – which helps meditation, which in turn is an aid to remembering the mantram.

The disciplines of this eight-point program cover every aspect of our inner and outer life, our relationships with other people as well as our own physical and emotional well-being. By practicing all these disciplines together, we keep our inner and outer life in balance. Meditation is turning inward, and it needs to be balanced with plenty of physical exercise, with work which demands our complete attention, and with association with other people. A good deal of energy is released in meditation, and there can sometimes be trouble if this energy is not harnessed during the rest of the day. As long as we are practicing the other disciplines sincerely, we are sure to put this energy to good use.

As we enter deeper stages of consciousness in meditation, it is really like entering a jungle. We may come face to face with the tigers that prowl in the unconscious: an old fear, a deep-seated hostility, or a fierce compulsion. If we are practicing all the disciplines together, the timing works out very nicely: we will develop the concentration necessary to get to the tiger's lair at the same time that we have the detachment and the will to fight it, not before. This is why it is so dangerous to try shortcuts into the unconscious, such as powerful drugs or occult breathing exercises; you can be catapulted right into the tiger's lair before you have any equipment to fight or protect yourself. In practical terms this can mean coming back to the surface level with a compulsion which will haunt you day and night, or perhaps getting trapped at a deeper level where you live in a dreamworld of your own. So these disciplines are meant to safeguard us, and I never recommend the practice of meditation without the allied disciplines.

In the eight-point program I teach, the mantram plays a unique role as the bridge between the interior discipline of meditation and the other, external disciplines, for it helps greatly in applying the power gained in meditation to the other disciplines throughout the day. Meditation is like a big, lays down a track into the depths of our consciousness. The mantram travels this track like one of those handcars railway men use in India: two men push a lever back and forth a few times to get the handcar started; then, once it picks up speed, it rolls on effortlessly down the line. In railway work this handcar can be a very convenient way to get from one place to another, and in the same way we can use the mantram handcar to bring the resources we tap in meditation into play in our lives throughout the day. Then, when we find ourselves provoked or worried or driven by some compulsive habit, just remembering the mantram will enable us to recall a little of the inner strength we glimpsed that morning in meditation.

In this way, the mantram can give the day real continuity. At the beginning, it may only extend your morning meditation a little into breakfast. You may have felt at peace with the whole world in your meditation room, but when you sit down to burned toast and cold coffee, that is the end of your patience for the day. Gradually, however, as your meditation deepens and you try your best to remember the mantram at every possible moment, it will extend your morning meditation into your mid-morning break, then to your lunch hour, and eventually into the afternoon. Finally, if you are practicing these disciplines sincerely, systematically, and with sustained enthusiasm, the mantram will enable you to take up your evening meditation exactly where you left off that morning. A lot of papers may have passed over your desk since your morning meditation; people may have interrupted you and irritated you and even spoken harshly to you; but if you have you and even spoken harshly to you; but if you have remembered the mantram whenever possible, none of these things will leave any agitation in your mind. And if you make a similar effort to fall asleep in the mantram that night, it will be an unbroken thread throughout your sleep connecting your evening meditation with the next morning's. When this happens, it is a sure sign that you are beginning to make progress towards being established in the mantram permanently.

I must confess that in talking about all these spiritual disciplines, I have been unable to hide my partiality for meditation. But meditation is hard, hard work. It is a tremendous challenge, and in the latter stages of meditation, we are tested to the very limits of our endurance. I am not trying to scare anyone off; the truth is that many people, especially the young, respond enthusiastically to meditation all the more when I tell them how difficult it is and how much it demands. But of course there are many people who are not willing to make this kind of commitment. To such people I always hasten to add that the spiritual life is a come-as-you-are party; we all start from where we are. If you are not prepared to meditate, you can still benefit greatly from the practice of the other disciplines. Any step you take towards the Self within will bring you increased vitality, greater security, and richer relations with those around you. No matter what your background, you will benefit if you repeat the mantram at odd moments during the day or when you are walking or falling asleep, and you will benefit even more if the mantram enables you to slow down, to become more one-pointed, and to put others first.

CHAPTER TWELVE

Becoming Established in the Mantram

THE MORE YOU use the mantram with regularity and dedication, the deeper it sinks into your consciousness. After many years of practice, when you have made considerable progress towards gaining mastery over the mind, you may become established in the mantram. Then it has become an integral part of your consciousness. You no longer have to make an effort to repeat it; it goes on repeating itself in the depths of your consciousness. The joy of this state has to be experienced to be described; it purifies the mind, brings us peace, and fills us with a quiet certainty that we are adequate to any challenge life may bring our way.

THE UNSTRUCK SOUND

There is a verse from the Hindu scriptures which says, "Sound produced from within is known as *anahata,* or 'unstruck.' Struck sound is said to give pleasure. Unstruck sound gives illumination." The sounds produced in music, however great, however beautiful, are all struck sounds. They are created by striking together two or more objects. They are not eternal. The drum or the violin or the cello or the cymbals are struck, and a sound is produced. But the mantram, the cosmic sound heard in the depths of consciousness, is a different kind of sound altogether. It is uncreated, eternal.

When in the Zen tradition they talk about "the clapping of one hand," that is what they are referring to: uncreated sound, sound which is "unstruck." One of the great joys of deep meditation is hearing this unstruck sound, which is represented by the syllable *Om*. But *Om* is just an approximation of what this uncreated sound is like. It is like no other sound on earth – that is the real meaning behind the image of the "unstruck" sound.

The Indian poet and mystic Kabir says, "In the cave of the heart, joy reigns ever. Music swells without an instrument." I am a lover of music, but there is no comparison between the music that I can hear in the depths of meditation and any symphony played by any orchestra. When he heard it, Saint Francis said that if it had continued a little longer his life would have melted away.

When, after many years of meditation, you hear this inner music for the first time, the joy is so great you cannot imagine how tremendous the impact is until you have the experience for yourself. It is the signal that you are about to enter the city of God within. Hearing this cosmic sound brings many benefits. It can put an end to compulsive attachment; it can wean you away from serious addictions; it can reduce your self-will;

it can bring great security to your mind and a radiance to your personality.

THE MANTRAM AFTER YEARS OF REPETITION

From the very first day you begin to use the mantram, it begins to grow in your consciousness. It germinates like the tiny seed that will eventually grow into a magnificent tree, and as you repeat it often and enthusiastically, it sends its roots deeper and deeper. Over a period of many years, if you have been practicing all the other spiritual disciplines which strengthen your will and deepen your concentration, the taproot of the mantram will extend fathoms deep, where it works to unify your consciousness – resolving old conflicts, solving problems you may not even be aware of, and transforming negative emotions into spiritual energy.

Finally, when this mantram root reaches the bedrock of consciousness, you become established in the mantram. It has become an integral part of your being, permeating your consciousness from the surface level down to the very depths. Then it is no longer necessary to repeat the mantram; it goes on repeating itself, echoing continuously at the very deepest levels of the mind. This is what Saint Paul means when he exhorts us to "pray without ceasing." As a Sufi mystic says,

Those who heard this word by the ear alone let it go
out by the other ear; but those who heard it with their
souls imprinted it on their souls and repeated it until

it penetrated their hearts and souls, and their whole being became this word.

In more homely language, it is as if after all these years of knocking – repeating the mantram assiduously whenever we get the chance – the mantram finally opens its doors and lets us in.

Becoming established in the mantram is one of the many marvelous developments which take place towards the very end of the spiritual journey, as we draw near to realizing the supreme goal of life. At this point, as the Sufi mystics put it beautifully, there is only one thin veil remaining between us and God, the Beloved. We can already make out the outlines of our real nature – abiding joy, unshakable security, and infinite love. But we do not reach this state overnight. We must have been repeating the mantram as often and as sincerely as we can for many years; and for the vast majority of us, we must have been practicing meditation sincerely and systematically also. Even then, the mystics of all religions tell us, we cannot become completely established in the mantram except through what I can only call divine grace. We must put in the effort; otherwise the Beloved will not take us seriously. But in the end it is only he – or she, as Sri Ramakrishna would say of the Divine Mother – who will open the doors of the holy name and take us in.

THE SECURITY OF THE MANTRAM

When this happens, there is a marvelous sense of security that comes, for you know that the mantram can never let you down. It has taken root deep in your consciousness, and as soon as a negative emotion begins to arise, the mantram automatically transforms it into tremendous positive power. For my mechanically minded friends, I sometimes say this is like having a transformer inside with a thermostat attached. When a negative emotion like fear or anger begins to rise, the thermostat sends the message, "Things are getting a little hot down here," and the mantram transformer switches on. Most of us become aware of these negative emotions only after they have risen to the surface level of consciousness, when they have gathered tremendous momentum. But the mantram transformer intercepts fear and anger and greed while they are still in the formative stages, deep in the unconscious, and converts them immediately into immense constructive power. This is why Saint Bernard of Clairvaux calls the mantram "the energizing Word."

When you have managed to become established in the mantram like this, there are really no negative emotions left; every little cranny of consciousness has been flooded with light. There are no selfish desires anywhere, hiding in the basement or in the back of a little cubbyhole of the mind; there are only selfless desires for the welfare of all. It is not that you have no feelings at this stage: if I may say so, it is only at this stage that you really know what sensitivity is, because you are so close to the unity of life that you feel the joy and suffering of everyone around you as your own. The difference is that now, grief or sorrow at the suffering of others opens the door to deeper resources for alleviating that suffering, and you will know without a doubt that you will be able to make a contribution to life.

WHEN CONCENTRATION BECOMES NATURAL

All spiritual disciplines converge by the time we reach this state, just as all the great religions converge for those who have realized God in their own consciousness. At this stage – but only at this stage – there is very little difference between repetition of the mantram and meditation and total concentration on something outside, because our consciousness is unified from the surface to the very depths. Then concentration is our natural state, and it becomes effortless and natural to focus our complete attention on anything we are doing. When we are talking to someone, we see no one but him, hear no one but her; and when we give our complete attention like this, people cannot help but respond. We can turn our attention to any problem and penetrate to the heart of it, which is the secret of genius in any field. Now, however, we will see only the unity of life, and all our energy will be directed to solving the biggest problems the world faces today – violence, the despoliation of the environment, the disintegration of the family.

Sri Ramakrishna tells us that being established in the mantram is like receiving a pension after many years of faithful service. When a professor retires as professor emeritus, his pay is sent regularly to his home. He still has a little pigeonhole on the campus where his mail comes, but he doesn't have to do any work if he doesn't want to, like grading examinations or sitting on committees. In my university days in India, I knew a few of these professors emeriti who were more regular than many of the regular professors. When you are a regular professor, you sometimes feel a little reluctant to go to the campus or sit down to work, because you know that you have got to do it. But when you become professor emeritus there is no one to compel you to work, so you are free to work just for the joy of it. You come in regularly, you get your pay, you have your privileges and your honors, but you don't have any responsibilities. Similarly, when you become established in the mantram, the Self, whose employees we all are, says, "You have been working all these years, repeating the mantram and observing the other disciplines from nine to five and at night and on weekends too. You can sit back now, and I will repeat the mantram for you."

Of course, like the professor emeritus, you can still repeat the mantram consciously if you like; the Self will not dock your pay. Shankara, a great mystic of medieval India, says that when you repeat the mantram consciously like this after becoming established in it, when you have nothing further to gain for yourself, the mantram is credited to those to whom you want the credit to go. You repeat your mantram, and those around you will find themselves a little more selfless, a little more secure.

LETTING THE MANTRAM INSIDE

Of course, these marvelous developments do not take place overnight. They take a long time, but the mantram begins its work of purifying our consciousness long before we reach the unitive state. At first, most of the work goes into trying to open the door of our mind a little so that the mantram can slip in. Once it gets in under the surface level, it can go on with its work of purification even when we are not consciously repeating it. But at first, it is all we can do to open the door of the mind even a little crack. All the time that we are repeating the mantram at the post office, while walking, while washing dishes, while falling asleep, we are working away at opening that door to our consciousness. When we can use the mantram to overcome likes and dislikes or to change old habits, we are beginning to open the door just a little, and when we learn to repeat the mantram to transform fear and anger and greed, we are not only opening the door but turning on the porch light and putting out the welcome mat too.

Once the mantram gets its foot in the door, it looks around inside and sees what a messy housekeeper the ego is. The ego doesn't dust, it doesn't sweep, and it can't stand to throw anything out, so our consciousness is bulging with photo albums, old projects we lost interest in halfway through, tapes of agitated conversations with our friends twelve years ago, even old childhood toys. The mantram slips inside and begins to straighten up the living room; it clears out the cobwebs, throws out the old magazines, and opens up all the windows to let in a little fresh air. Compared to this, those stables Hercules had to clean were like the house beautiful, but gradually the mantram will go through everything room by room. Only when the entire house is spotless from cellar to attic is it ready for its rightful owner: your real Self.

A FEW WONDERFUL SIGNS

Even in the early days, there are several sure signs that the mantram has begun its work of purification. One sign is that you will hear the mantram occasionally in your sleep, either in a dream or in the state of dreamless sleep. In a dream, the mantram can save you from all sorts of unpleasant situations. Perhaps you have always been afraid of Dracula and sometimes dream that he is pursuing you. You try to run but your legs get heavier and heavier, as if you were wading through quicksand. The panic mounts. Just then you hear the mantram and Dracula disappears, along with all sense of fear. The mantram has come to your rescue, and not just to save you from one unpleasant incident; it is quite likely that this particular fear has disappeared from your consciousness permanently.

Sometimes, too, you may hear the mantram echoing deep in your consciousness, not necessarily in connection with any dream. It will have an unearthly beauty and clarity which will haunt you when you wake up. During the following day you will not be able to recapture just how it sounded in all its beauty, but the mere memory of it will fill you with joy and security. This will give you added incentive to try harder in all your spiritual disciplines, because you know that sustained effort is what really enables you to drive the mantram deep into your consciousness. But there is a danger here of dwelling on such experiences and getting elated over them. For a long, long time they will be like angels' visits, few and far between. So let me suggest that you regard experiences like these not as experiences to be sought in themselves, but only as a sign that the mantram is gradually sinking into your consciousness. Even if you never hear the mantram in your sleep, as long as you are looking for opportunities during the day to repeat it, especially in training the senses and putting others first, you can be sure that it is taking root.

When you hear the mantram in your sleep, you are not consciously repeating it; this is the mantram at work on a deeper level of consciousness. To become established in the mantram, you must be able to repeat it consciously far below the surface level of thought and action. For this to take place, I cannot stress too much how important it is to make use of every opportunity during the day and night to repeat the mantram. Even then, it is not just the number of times you have said the mantram which takes you to a deeper level but the sincerity and enthusiasm with which you say it as well, combined with the other spiritual disciplines like meditation. I have no hesitation in saying that you cannot become established in the mantram unless you have also reduced your self-will to a very considerable extent. These two go together. Self-will is devotion to "I," which the mantram transforms into devotion to God.

THE PRESENCE OF GOD

When we have unified our consciousness through these powerful disciplines, not only do meditation and the mantram come together, but all mantrams come together too. Whether our mantram is *Rama, Rama* or *Jesus, Jesus* or *Hail Mary* or *Om mani padme hum,* it fills us with the same joy and security, and it reverberates in the depths of our consciousness with the same beauty. There is a beautiful hymn in Sanskrit called *The Thousand Names of the Lord,* meant to inspire us with a thousand divine attributes of the supreme reality we call God. Many of these names are used as mantrams in the Hindu tradition, but great mystics like Gandhi have proved in their lives that all these thousand holy names are contained in the single name *Rama,* as mentioned in the scriptures. This is to tell us that once the mantram has become an integral part of our consciousness, all mantrams are the same. Whatever holy name we use, at this stage it is the perfect embodiment of the Lord of Love.

The holy name reverberating in the depths of consciousness transfigures our entire vision of life. Just as the mantram transforms negative forces in consciousness into constructive power, so it now transforms all our perceptions of the everyday world into unbroken awareness of the unity of life. When I go for a walk on the beach my ear hears the waves crashing and booming against the shore, but my mind hears them as *Rama, Rama, Rama.* This is not something I try to do; it's simply how I hear it now. And when I hear the birds singing, their song too becomes *Rama, Rama, Rama* – with different accents, with different harmonies, but the final perception is the holy name. It is the same with the breeze, with music, with everything. As Swami Ramdas says, the name *is* God, not a symbol but reality; and when we are established in the mantram, established in awareness of God, everything is full of Rama – full of joy.

Index

THE BLUE MOUNTAIN CENTER OF MEDITATION

The Blue Mountain Center of Meditation publishes Easwaran's books, videos, and audios, and offers retreats on his eight-point program of passage meditation. For more information:

The Blue Mountain Center of Meditation
Box 256, Tomales, California 94971
Telephone: +1 707 878 2369
Toll-free in the US: 800 475 2369
Facsimile: +1 707 878 2375
Email: info@easwaran.org
www.easwaran.org

NILGIRI PRESS

THE BOOKS OF EKNATH EASWARAN

TIMELESS WISDOM

Timeless Wisdom: Passages for Meditation from the World's Saints & Sages offers a collection of spiritual texts selected by Eknath Easwaran expressly for meditation.

This rich anthology includes passages from all the world's traditions, some familiar and others less well known but equally beautiful. Here are flashes of insight from the Hindu Upanishads, prayers of comfort from the Christian saints, psalms from the Jewish scriptures, songs of praise from the Sufis, deep wisdom from the Buddhist and Taoist traditions.

NILGIRI PRESS

THE BOOKS OF EKNATH EASWARAN

PASSAGE MEDITATION

"This is the secret of meditation: we become what we meditate on."
 – Eknath Easwaran

This companion volume to *Timeless Wisdom* is an introduction to Easwaran's method of meditation, in which we choose inspirational passages that embody our highest ideals and send them deep into consciousness through slow, sustained attention. Our passages become lifelines, taking us to the source of wisdom deep within and then guiding us through the challenges of daily life.

Universal and dogma-free, passage meditation is part of Easwaran's eight-point program of practical skills. Based on traditional spiritual practices but adjusted for modern lifestyles, *Passage Meditation* goes step by step through each point of Easwaran's program, showing us how to stay calm and focused at work and at home.

NILGIRI PRESS

Publisher's Cataloging-In-Publication Data

(Prepared by The Donohue Group, Inc.)

Easwaran, Eknath.

  The mantram handbook : a practical guide to choosing your
mantram & calming your mind / Eknath Easwaran ; foreword by
Daniel Lowenstein. -- 5th ed.

  p. ; cm.

  Includes index.

  ISBN: 978-1-58638-028-1

1. Mantras. 2. Spiritual life. I. Lowenstein, Daniel (Daniel Henry),
1953- II. Title.

BL624 .E17 2009

294.5/43

2008931228